# Three Flags and Two Brothers

## *To War and Back*

### By

# Holly E. Rees

an imprint of Event Horizon Publishing Group
Bryan, Texas 2016

# Three Flags and Two Brothers: to War and Back

Copyright © 2016 by Holly E. Rees
All Rights Reserved.

Without limiting the rights under copyright reserved above, no part of this book may be reproduced in any form or by any electronic or mechanical means, including information storage and retrieval systems, without written permission from the author, except by a reviewer who may quote brief passages in review.

Published by Lone Star Publishing
an imprint of Event Horizon Publishing Group
4103 S. Texas Avenue, Suite 219-A
Bryan, Texas 77802
eventhorizonpg.com

Book and Cover design by
Thomas Knowles, Caitlin Pratt and Crystal Wolfe

ISBN 13: 978-0-9794354-5-4
ISBN10: 0-9794354-5-5

First Lone Star Publishing Edition: October 2016

PRINTED IN THE USA

# DEDICATION

To the foot soldiers of World War II,
both Army and Marines,
this book is solemnly dedicated.

## SPECIAL THANKS

A very personal and heartfelt thank-you to my dear friend and prayer partner, Exa York, for all her encouragement and much work in getting my book written and manuscript typed, with occasional editorial suggestions. Special thanks also to Linda Wickman for typing and correcting much of the manuscript and to the other ladies from St. Luke's United Methodist Church who helped out with the typing: Louise Davis, Terry Davis, Tonya Lyons, Loueva Clark and Melba Madison.

Thanks, too, to Anna at CVS Pharmacy for her help with pictures and to Dawn at Wal-Mart Portrait Studio for the pictures she took, also to Judy at Kinkos. Thanks to Mike Southerland for his encouragement and for taking some pictures. Special thanks to my son, two daughters, and daughter-in-law, Brenda for their love, support, encouragement, help, prayers and patience.

Additional thanks to Mike Estrada for his help in getting Gil's Navy records.

It is my sincere desire that any royalties or profit that may accrue to me from the sale of this book will be paid to the National World War II Museum in New Orleans, the National Army Museum in Virginia, the National Infantry Museum in Georgia, and the Pacific War Museum in Fredericksburg, Texas, in equal amounts.

# The Three Flags

Upper Right: The U.S. WWII Blue Star Service Flag —
Displayed in windows of homes to indicate the
number of family members in service during the war

Center: The **Hinomaru Yosegoui** —
an individual Japanese silk flag inscribed with
personal messages in Kanji characters, carried by
Japanese Infantryman Tomoe Sanshi on Okinawa

Lower Left: The Flag of the United States of America —
folded as by tradition at the close of a funeral for
one who has served in the armed forces.

# The Brothers

### Gilbert and Holly Rees
#### Navy and Army

#### November 1944
#### Van Nuys, California

#### Gil was just back from the sinking of the **USS Princeton**; Holly was on weekend leave from Camp Roberts.

# Table of Contents

**PART ONE:   PRE-MILITARY** ........................................................... 1
    1 Family ........................................................................ 3
    2 Pre-Induction ........................................................... 17

**PART TWO:   MILITARY SERVICE** ..................................... 21
    3 Induction and Basic Training ....................................... 23
    4 Leave and Rout to Okinawa ........................................ 33
    5 Infantry Company Weapons & Equipment ............... 39
    6 Combat on Okinawa .................................................... 65
    7 Wounded, Hospital and Rehab .................................... 83
    8 The 7th Infantry on Okinawa:
       Combat Observations ................................................ 91
    9 Post-Hospital Military ................................................. 97
    10 U.S. Navy Aircraft Carriers & Aircraft .................... 107
    11 Gilbert Rees, Navy 1942—1949 ................................ 119

**COLOR ALBUM** ................................................................ 140

**PART THREE: POST MILITARY LIFE** ..................................... 151
    12 Gilbert Rees—Post-Navy ............................................ 153
    13 Holly Rees—Post-Infantry ......................................... 159
    14 Family ........................................................................ 164
    15 Employment to Retirement ....................................... 175
    16 Church, Faith, and Religion ....................................... 181
    17 Avocations and Public Service .................................. 187
    18 Health and Care Giving ............................................. 195

**PART FOUR: CONFLICTS AND RESOLUTIONS** .............. 201
    19 Return to Okinawa .................................................... 203
    20 Honoring Death: The Rising Sun Flag ..................... 229
    21 On Combat, Killing, and Forgiveness ....................... 233

## MAPS & AERIAL PHOTOGRAPHS
Countour Map of Okinawa pgs. 62-63   U.S. Operations on Okinawa p. 64
Map of Southern Okinawa p. 67   Advance on Shuri p. 68   Closing in on Shuri, May 1945 p. 70
Sugar Loaf Hill & Horseshoe Hill p.72   Final Battles, Okinawa p.79

# Foreword

To write or not to write, that is the question. For several years I have been wrestling with the idea of writing a book about my World War II experiences. I kept coming up with reasons to and not to, and finally, as I pass my 90th birthday, I think the pros outweigh the cons.

Part of the concern is that writing about oneself seems like the ultimate ego trip. Since I don't think of myself as a "hero" or certainly not a military historian, why write? On the other hand, I have had experiences that no one else has had, and if I don't write them down, no one else can or will.

Being 90 and 71 years after the Battle for Okinawa, with a little inertia probably thrown in, could easily be a deterrent. However, this could also be a plus factor since memories are still vivid and clear. What I don't know now I probably didn't know then either. We didn't have nametags, wore no insignia, had no outside radio, newspapers, magazines, could not keep diaries (Sledge not withstanding) and so had little information or communication.

We were informed of the death of President and Commander in Chief Franklin Roosevelt, Victory in Europe and the sinking of the Yamato and General Buckner's death by Army radio and word of mouth, mostly though we existed, or rather survived, in our own little world at the Infantry Company level.

With some variations, of course, I am impressed with the similarities between my experiences and observations in I Company 184th Infantry, 7th Division and those written about by Sledge, Sloan and Green and even those illustrated in *Saving Private Ryan*, *Band of Brothers* and *The War* (Ken Burns).

I have some 30 books, half books or books with a chapter on Okinawa as well as articles and 25 other books on general or other World War II subjects. Thus, it would seem that any more would be overkill and redundant. However, most are by historians about the battles and few are by participants. I have only one book by a Japanese (Yahara), one by an Okinawan (Ota), one by a Marine (Sledge) and one by an Army tanker (Green) with *none* by an Army infantryman. Of the historical writings, they tend to run about 75 percent about Marine activities and about 25 percent on the Army—although they purport to tell about "all the major battles on Okinawa."

Many of my brothers in arms never made it back or have died since and can never record their experiences. Therefore, I feel a solemn obligation to speak for them as well as tell my own story.

I have been urged by several people to write this account, especially Dr. Don Miller and my son, Lane Rees.

After reading Sledge's *With the Old Breed* and Burchett's *Last Light* (a poignant account of a preacher's wife and her gradual succumbing to the ravages of Alzheimer's Disease), I told my youngest daughter, "I could have written those. They closely parallel my own situations and experiences." Her reply was, "Well, why don't you? It's never too late."

As I was recently going through some boxes in my garage, looking for the books I have by Ernie Pyle and Bill Mauldin, I came across a treasure trove of papers and memorabilia of my late brother, Gil. I was very interested in and impressed by his service in the Navy (some of which I knew about and some I didn't). Suddenly I had an epiphany that I should write about the Rees brothers.

When I was recently reading Bob Green's book, *Okinawa Odyssey*, I was frustrated with the lengthy history about his grandfather, father, the Green Ranch, his boyhood and going to New Mexico Military Institute prior to his Army experiences. Later I came to realize that we are all a product of our family and life experiences. Thus, this background information helps me to know a lot more about Bob Green the tanker.

So, I am including probably more than you want to know about our lives before World War II, our experiences during the war, and some of the post-war information. This information will, collectively, give you a better picture of who we are.

I need to apologize early on for the obvious imbalance between writings about Gil and myself. Since I am writing this book and since he died young (at 28 in 1953), I know a lot more about myself than about him. I cannot obtain much more about his life (although I did get his Navy records from the government storage center in St. Louis) but thought it important to include his life story and what I do know.

When I was in combat on Okinawa at the young age of 19, I had absolutely no qualms about killing the Japanese. Later, after becoming a Christian, I had periods of remorse. I knew I was forgiven and that killing in wartime combat is not like killing in civilian life. I have been back and forth on this and generally conclude that it's water under the bridge, cannot be changed, and have moved on with life.

It is a miracle that the process of war can take young, good, ordinary men out of society and transform them into such efficient killers. Another miracle is that society can integrate the survivors back as good, ordinary people. The greatest miracle is that anyone could survive the living hell of the carnage of war. But we did, and this, then, is our story.

# SHOCK TROOPER

There is pride in each branch of the forces,
    From boot camp to far oversea,
A pride whose ebullient source is
    The spirit of men who are free;
But the pride that is tallest and deepest
    Is that of the battle-wise clan
Whose lives are the toughest—and cheapest,

    The pride of the Combat Man.
No matter how long or how much is
    The task of support and supply,
He knows, when it comes to the clutches,
    That he is the Ultimate Guy:
The spearhead, the bludgeon, the hammer,
    Expended "according to plan"
But wrapped in that grim, gutful glamour,

    The pride of the Combat Man.
It's a pride that is utterly stranger
    To phrases of splendor and fire.
He knows that the "Bright Face of Danger"
    Is blackened with blood and with mire.
And only he fronts the cold glare in
    The bleak eyes of Fate he must scan;
So—none but his buddies can share in

    The pride of the Combat Man.
It's a pride that keeps hopeless men trying
    Whom no other power can drive,
It's a pride in the will to face dying
    And to sweat and to freeze—and survive;
A pride that's the basic, eternal
    Hard core of that strange, aloof clan—
The heart and the marrow and kernel
    And soul of the Combat Man!

                  (by Berton Braley)

# Part One

## Pre-Military

# 1

## FAMILY

*"On Sunday morning, December 7, 1941, a friend of mine, Wilbur Thorpe, came over to see me and told me that the Japanese had attacked Pearl Harbor. We sat in his Plymouth coupe and listened to the radio and barely recognized the effect this would have on all our lives over the next four years—and even for life."*

OUR PATERNAL GRANDFATHER, ELIAS REES (for whom I am named) was born February 22, 1871, in Merthyr Tydfil, Gelligan County of Glamorgan, Wales, United Kingdom. He immigrated to the United States with his parents, Enoch and Ann Rees, and his siblings, when he was nine.

On March 24, 1897, Elias married Minnie Prothero (whose parents, William and Elizabeth Prothero, were also born in Wales). They were married in Plymouth, Pennsylvania, but soon left the anthracite coalmines to move to the Southwest to work in the copper, gold, and silver mines. Their first-born son, Gilbert Enoch Rees, was born on February 17, 1901, in Hedges, California. (This was a mining camp and no longer exists.)

Our maternal grandfather, Marion Holly, was born July 15, 1868, in Bradford County, Pennsylvania, to Silas and Harriett Holly. Marion married Julia Williams in the late 1890s. Their second child was Hazel Marion Holly, who was born March 5, 1903, in Fulton, Missouri.

Gilbert Rees and Hazel Holly were married January 1, 1923, in Phoenix, Arizona. Gilbert was an automobile mechanic and later an automotive machinist. Before he married he built and raced racecars. After a near-fatal accident he gave up racing, but kept on building racecars. Later, he rebuilt Offenhauser engines, and one year he had five "Offies" racing at Indianapolis (in race cars).

Dad was an avid fisherman and hunter. He was an accomplished do-it-yourselfer who could do almost anything but who knew when to call in the expert. I have many fond memories (and a very deep appreciation for the training and example) of helping him with cement work, carpentry, plumbing, electrical, fencing, welding, metalwork, roofing, etc. and of course auto mechanics.

During World War II after I went into the Army and Gil was already in the Navy, Mom and Dad moved to the San Fernando Valley in California. They both worked for Sturdivant Auto Parts and Machine Shop. Mom was a bookkeeper and Dad was shop foreman.

In 1947 Mom and Dad moved back to Prescott and he started his own business, Rees Motor Rebuild. I spent the summer of 1947 helping him get the garage and equipment set up. He had equipment to bore cylinders, grind valves, do in-car crank shaft grinding, make bearings, plus lathe, welding, etc. He did this until he semi-retired at 65.

Gilbert Enoch Rees, Jr. was born July 24, 1924, at the Mercy Hospital in Prescott, Yavapai County, Arizona. Besides being named for his father, the Enoch was our great-grandfather's name.

HOLLY AND GILBERT REES, 1929

I was born Holly Elias Rees, January 21, 1926, at the same place. My given name is my mother's maiden name, and my middle name is my grandfather's name.

If Gil and I were Japanese we would be known as "Nisei," or second-generation native born, whose grandparents were foreign-born immigrants.

When we were quite young, they called Gil "Sonny Rees" since he was a junior. My mom would get us together to teach us what to say and do if we got lost, etc. She would say to Gil, "What is your name, little boy?" and he would answer "Nunny Wees." She then asked me my name and I would answer, "Nunny's widow brudder."

Our surname, Rees, is very common in Wales, but most people want to add an "e" and spell it Reese. My Uncle Dave got so tired of telling people, he just added an "e" himself, which was a major irritation for his mother, my grandmother.

My personal burden was being stuck with a female first name. Mom had a male first cousin, Holly Darling Betts (who always went by H. D.) and she insisted that it was both a male and female name. H. D. was the only other male I have ever known and/or heard of with the name Holly. I have run into a few, but they are usually nicknames for Hollister, Holloway or something else. I always was told that I was going to be Holly Rees whether I was a girl or a boy.

My first major test was when I graduated from high school and most of the major girls' colleges (Smith, Wellesley, Vassar, etc.) contacted me to attend. "A Boy Named Sue" was something I could relate to. Probably half or more of the mail I have received in my lifetime is addressed as Miss, Mrs. or Ms.

One time I had a date with a girl named Johnnie. We were in a restaurant and introductions were being made, and we were introduced as Holly and Johnnie. The guy turned to me and said, "Nice meeting you, Johnny" and I had to say, "No, no, I'm Holly—she's Johnnie."

In the Army we had countless roll calls in which the sergeant would call out last name and you would yell out your first name and middle initial in response, i.e., "Rees"—"Holly E," which was always embarrassing.

The Social Security Administration usually paired us up in hotels when we went to meetings to save money and to have us get better acquainted. I can remember a number of times that I had reservations to share a room with a female SSA employee and how the hotel would scramble to get things changed. It was also frustrating to get mail addressed to Miss, Mrs., Ms. when the writer should have known I was a male.

After Betty and I married, we also had an interesting routine in our home. Most phone calls were for me so I tried to answer the phone. The caller, with the name Holly Rees, assumed a female. So, when I would answer, they'd ask to speak to Mrs. Rees. I'd call for Betty and say: "It's for you." Then she'd get on the phone and find out they wanted me and say, "No, it's for you."

Besides having a feminine first name, my initials are H.E.R. which doesn't do anything to make the situation any more masculine. When I was in college I bought a box (3) of Pima cotton white dress shirts with French cuffs. The store embroidered my initials on the left cuff. Some of my friends would look on the right cuff to see if it said "his"!

A distant cousin on my mother's side was former Arizona Governor George W. P. Hunt. At one time (and as far as I know still stands) he held the U.S. record for the most terms as a governor (seven). He was governor when Arizona became a state in 1912 and for six consecutive terms. Later he was U.S. ambassador to Siam in the late 20s-early 30s and still later served a seventh term as governor. I have a blue sapphire ring that he sent my Grandmother Holly from Siam, also, a Christmas card from 1914 and several postcards he sent her.

Both Gil and I had a fairly normal and uneventful elementary school experience. One we shared was when the entire school system met at the high school to welcome native son Fiorela La Guardia on a visit (long-time mayor of New York City for whom La Guardia Terminal is named). Another time I tried out for and was selected for a child role in the high school annual Christmas play. Miss Lillian Savage, the high school speech and drama teacher, to help alleviate stage fright, told us to imagine we were sitting on a fence in front of a cabbage patch, and that the audience was made up of cabbage heads. Many times since then I have recalled this suggestion and noticed the similarity.

After I finished the first grade I was sick and stayed out of school for a year and had treatment and recuperation and resumed second grade the next year. I did well and later the question came up about skipping a year and catching up with the class I had started with. The teacher recommended against it, and I never did.

I always had a love of reading, and would ride my bike to the public library and bring home books to read. In junior high school I was picked to be the editor of the Freshman Page of the *Badger* called the "Underpup."

During our high school years we always had, or had access to, a workshop and tools, and so we did well in shop classes. At home we had tinker toys, erector sets, chemistry sets, World Book Encyclopedia and many other books. We also had scooters and bicycles and loved to hike and explore the outdoors. We usually had a pet dog to love and care for. We also had chores to do.

Since I was sickly and smaller, Gil usually got the chore to rake, mow, weed, etc. outdoors. His solution was to break (accidentally) the handle. Dad would replace the handle with a bigger, heavier one, sometimes even metal pipe. So, when I started the outdoor chores the rake, hoe and shovel were sturdy and heavy and not easily broken.

Gil was mean to me and seemed to go out of his way to pick on me and make my life miserable. Two examples come to mind. One was when he burned me on the arm with a cigarette. Another was when I made a celestial telescope. I bought a kit with the lenses and made the tube from the center of a roll of newsprint (cardboard). Gil took the garden hose and filled up the telescope with water, which of course ruined it. I used to dream of the day when I grew up and I would beat the living tar out of him. When he left for the Navy I was 16 and just finished my sophomore year in high school and wasn't near that point yet. By the time I finished "Killer Kollege" (Infantry Basic Training), I outweighed him and (I think) could have done the job. However, we both had mellowed, and I no longer had the desire for revenge.

Gil was plenty smart, but lazy and unmotivated, especially in school. He often just barely squeaked by, and one year our parents promised him a new bicycle if he passed (which he did). I was always on the Honor Roll with good grades and thought that I should have been rewarded, too.

I can't remember my mother ever laying a hand (or belt) on Gil or me. Rather she would tell us "wait 'til your Dad gets home," and the belt would come then. Usually the infraction was our fighting, and we often got over it and were playing peacefully by the time the belt was applied. Also the house rule was we both were presumed involved and guilty and both got the belt. It took having children of my own to convince me that this wasn't a bad policy, though I still think the delayed punishment wasn't good.

Even growing up in the depression, we always had a roof over our heads, adequate clothing, never missed a meal, etc. Extra money was tight. After I became a Boy Scout, I wanted a sheath knife, and saved my money and finally bought one. One day Gil got a hold of it and was throwing it at the coal shed and ended up breaking the tip off. I thought (think) that justice demanded Gil buy me a new knife, but Dad ground it and reshaped it for me. I still have that knife today.

When I reached high school as a sophomore, Gil was a senior and had already had a lot of the teachers that I would have. One, "Pop" McNary,

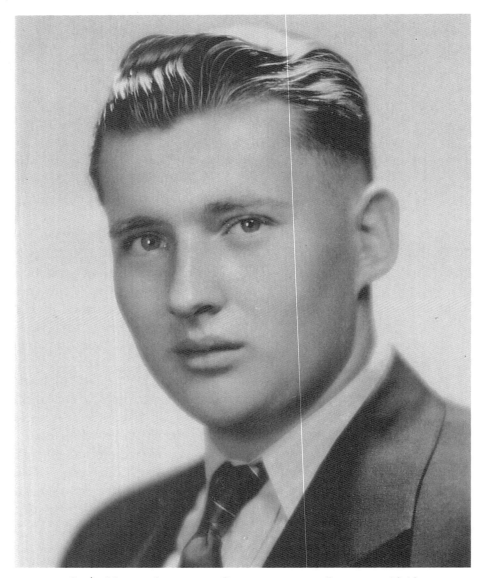

GIL'S HIGH SCHOOL GRADUATION PHOTO, 1942

taught plane geometry, and the first grade he gave me was a "C." I went to see him and told him he knew Gil but not me, and that I was going to ace the course, which I did.

I can't remember Gil going to a dance or having a date or showing any interest in the girls until after he went into the Navy. He did have guy friends that he enjoyed bumming around with. During high school he slept in a "storeroom" building out behind the house. I had the back bedroom. He would go out with the guys and they would bring him home and wait in the alley. He would come into the house, turn on the lights, slam the doors, flush the toilet at least once and then go out to his room. He would then hook the screen door from the inside, roll up pillows to look like he was in bed and then go out a window and rejoin his friends for the night's fun. He often came in late, but always before the family got up in the morning. Later, when I wanted to stay out late Mom would always chide me that Gil *always* came home and went to bed by 10:00 to 10:30. I'm not sure she ever believed me when I told her what he had done.

Some of Gil's friends were interested in radio, and that became his passion. Where he had been indifferent to studying, he suddenly got into radio. He studied, passed all the tests and paperwork and became a "ham radio operator." He fixed up his room as his station for the transmitter and built a large tower between his bedroom and mine as his antennae. He stayed home more then and often was on the radio late at night when reception was better. This was probably the best thing that ever happened to him, and he went on to graduate from high school and used this skill in the Navy. His amateur radio license was dated 08/30/41 and his station call number was W6UKB.

## PRESCOTT, ARIZ.
## W6UKB
### ARIZONA
### ★ Prescott

Radio.................... Tnx for the QSO
on............19......at.........M-MST
Ur........Mc.........sigs RST...........
Xmtr ...................................
Rcvr ....................................
PSE QSL OM           73           GILBERT REES JR. (Gil)

GIL'S HAM RADIO CARD W6UKB

On Sunday morning, December 7, 1941, a friend of mine, Wilbur Thorpe, came over to see me and told me that the Japs had attacked Pearl Harbor. We sat in his Plymouth coupe and listened to the radio and barely recognized the effect this would have on all our lives over the next four years—and even for life.

Gil went into the Navy after graduation, and we gradually began to see the war on the home front. There was a Negro Military Police camp at the county fairgrounds. Air Corps personnel from the valley would come up to the mountains. More and more of the guys would enlist, get drafted or get into defense work. We collected newspaper, aluminum, iron, tires and tubes and lived with rationing of food, gasoline, tires, etc.

I registered for the draft by my 18th birthday on January 21, 1944. Since I was already in my last semester of high school, I applied for a student deferment to finish high school and graduate. I will pick back up on this theme later in the chapter on my military service.

Unlike Gil, I loved to read and excelled in school, both studies and other activities, except sports. I was very near-sighted and wore glasses, and that didn't fit the sports scene. I pursued a college prep program in high school so I was prepared for any contingency.

I took Latin for two years, and have always been glad that I did, although I have often wished I knew Spanish, too. Plane geometry and chemistry took care of my math and science requirements. Although I took English every year, I think I learned more English in Latin class. History and civics, typing and bookkeeping were just routine.

Speech class was always a pleasure and also led to participation in debate and oratorical contests and major parts in plays in both junior and senior years. Journalism was also a special interest and I was the editor of the *Badger*, business manager of the *Hassagamper* and had membership in Quill and Scroll. I took and endured P.E., and one time coach "Ham" Pratt told me to get my grade from the Journalism teacher since I spent more time excused for a story than I did in P.E. I think he was partially serious.

I was the president of the Senior Class, which among other things called for me to lead the Grand March at the Junior-Senior Prom and the Processional and Recessional at both baccalaureate and graduation exercises.

At graduation I was dating one of the two pianists and so I marched in with one, and they switched, and I marched out with the other.

I was a member of the National Honor Society, and the "15" club (nine seniors and six juniors), both as a junior and as a senior. In 1943 I was named the Boys Merit Cup (aka outstanding boy) winner as a junior and

HOLLY'S HIGH SCHOOL GRADUATION PHOTO, 1944

again in 1944 as a senior. In Prescott High School history I am the only person to do so as a junior and as a two-time recipient.

At graduation I was named the male winner of the Danforth Award for Citizenship and Character. Best of all, I graduated as valedictorian of my class. We started high school with about 120 people, but some dropped out and went into the service, and we ended up with 89. Two of the perks that went with the honor were (1) a year's subscription from

*Readers Digest*. I got one copy before I went into the Army and never saw another. The other perk (2) was a four-year scholarship at the University of Arizona. The problem was it had to be started in 1944, and since I was almost certainly going to be in the service by then, the scholarship was given to a girl farther down the pecking order.

Both Gil and I were in the Boy Scouts (in different troops), and I feel that our training and experiences (such as camping) were of great value to us in the Army and Navy.

BOY SCOUT INFORMATION BOOTH, HOLLY REES 4TH FROM LEFT

For instance, one year at camp I won the marksmanship award (with 22 caliber rifle) and later ended up in infantry training and as a rifleman in infantry combat.

I started collecting coins in July 1935 when I was 9 years old and have been an avid numismatist for 81 years.

Gil was nominally interested in stamp collecting for a while, with the encouragement of our uncle, Silas Holly, who was an avid philatelist. This was never a real commitment and declined even more when he got involved in radio.

Holly at Boy Scout camp rifle range

Holly with coin collection

I did some yard work at home, especially after Gil went into the Navy, and occasionally some around the neighborhood. I was never too interested in this, nor had much time either.

My first real job was in the office of the *Prescott Courier*. I worked after school for a couple of hours in the early evening, selling newspapers over the counter, replenishing the supply for carriers and independent sellers, answering the phone for complaints about non-receipt and going to the archives to retrieve back copies. We kept a lot for 30 days and a smaller amount for a year. The editorial and office staff usually left shortly after I arrived, but the pressman, linotype operators, etc. were still working.

The *Courier* had a contract with and printed the *Arizona Highway Magazine* during this time. I met, and knew, Raymond Carlson, the editor of the *Arizona Highway Magazine*. This work at the newspaper started in junior high and extended into my high school years.

When I was a sophomore, I wanted to have a gold railroad watch (to tell time and probably show off). Obviously I didn't have the necessary money, so when I selected a Waltham 23 jewel beauty, I bought it on layaway. After paying half or more, the jeweler offered for me to take the watch and keep making weekly payments. I declined and waited until I had paid in full and it was mine to take possession. I was one proud dude when I sported the watch at school.

The summer of 1943 I worked at a Union Oil Station on the square in downtown Prescott owned by Dan Hankins. I pumped gas, did oil changes, fixed flats, made deliveries and was a general flunky. This was during rationing so we had that to deal with.

The summer of 1944, after graduating from high school, I got a job driving a dump truck for the Arizona Highway Department. I expected to be drafted any day but ended up working June, July and August. We did seal coats, patching, pick ups and a variety of jobs over the Prescott District that covered about a 50-mile radius.

Since most of the able-bodied men were in the service, we "boys" were asked to "volunteer" to serve in the Ground Observation Corps (to look for and report enemy aircraft—which I never saw over Arizona). In the same way we worked with Forest Fire Fighter (FFF) with the U.S. Forest Service.

When Gil got his social security card, he was working for the "BB Co." (Bashford-Burmister). This was a grocery store (where he worked) and a furniture and general merchandise store. This is the only job of his that I recall.

During WWII most civilian manufacturing and production was curtailed to utilize the facilities for war material. This was especially true for cars and trucks but also appliances, clothing, shoes, sports items, etc.

Many consumer items, besides being in short supply, were rationed. The federal government set up local ration boards where you went to apply for ration books of ration stamps.

Gasoline and petroleum products, as well as tires and tubes, were rationed on a needs basis—society needs, not personal. Many food items were also rationed, such as sugar, meat, butter, flour, etc. I remember margarine coming in a #1 plastic pouch. It was white and seemed like Crisco. There was a little capsule of coloring that you broke and kneaded the pouch until the color was mixed in and it looked like butter.

There were numerous collection drives for cardboard, newspapers, aluminum, iron, rubber and fat. These could be recycled and help meet the need for these materials.

I remember my dad added a second gas tank to our 1935 Studebaker sedan. This enabled us to increase the range of travel and adapt to the gasoline rationing.

Fighting the summer forest fires in the Prescott National Forest, we had some very interesting and hairy experiences with a number of large, medium and small fires.

Church was not a part of my life at that time—something I will address later.

I got interested in the girls and started dating in my junior year. We had learned to dance in gym class in junior high, but it took awhile for the interest to develop.

# ORDER TO REPORT FOR INDUCTION

## The President of the United States,

To    <u>Holly     Elias         Rees</u>
   (First name)   (Middle name)   (Last name)

## *GREETING:*

# 2

## PRE-INDUCTION

> *"We had a presumption that we would be in the Army very soon and would likely end up as cannon fodder in the European Theater of Operations."*

> *"When we hadn't been called (i.e., drafted) during June, July or August, my buddy Eugene "Gene" Hayes and I went to the draft board to volunteer."*

AS I MENTIONED EARLIER, I REGISTERED with the draft board when I turned 18. I requested and was granted a deferment to finish and graduate from high school. We graduated on a Friday night, June 3, 1944, and had to report to the induction station in Phoenix on Monday, June 6, for our pre-induction physicals.

As we gathered at the Prescott Post Office in the predawn hours, someone had a portable radio, and we received the news about "D Day," the Allied landing at Normandy. At that time we had a presumption that we would be in the Army very soon and would likely end up as "cannon fodder" in the European Theater of operations.

We loaded onto a charter bus and drove to Phoenix for a cursory physical. Shortly afterwards I received a written notice that I was "fit for duty."

After returning to Prescott, I got a job with the Arizona Highway Department as a dump truck driver with the understanding that I would be drafted soon.

Since my brother Gil had gone into the Navy as a seaman 1st class, received some college training in math and radio and always had a clean, warm, and dry place to sleep, I tried to get into the Navy. I read and studied for the test, and even though I wasn't that interested in radio I was sure I could learn and do what needed to be done. Before taking the test (which

I never did), I visited the Navy recruiter and he told me to "read that eye chart over there on the wall." I warily glanced at all four walls and finally said, "Which wall?" He said, "Son, the Navy doesn't want you, but the Army will." All the eye charts I had ever seen had the big "E" on top with gradually smaller letters underneath. The Navy eye chart had letters not over 5/8-inch high, and the distance you were from the chart to read it determined your visual acuity.

HOLLY'S PREINDUCTION PHYSICAL LETTER

When we hadn't been called (i.e., drafted) during June, July or August, my buddy Eugene "Gene" Hayes and I went to the draft board to volunteer. The technical term was "waive your draft status," and our draft numbers acquired a "V" after the number for "volunteer." Within a couple of weeks, we found ourselves back on a bus to Phoenix to the induction center. On September 23, 1944, we were sworn into the "Army of the United States."

I always thought I was in the U.S. Army and didn't know until I was discharged 21 months and 7 days later that there was a difference. It seems the United States Army is the "regular Army" and the draftee, citizens, war-time Army was the "Army of the United States."

HOLLY'S ORDER TO REPORT

# Part Two

## Military Service

# 3

## INDUCTION & BASIC TRAINING

*"Their goal was to whet our appetites to make us want to go forth and kill every one of them. This made it easier to evade the moral dilemma involved with the massive killing of war, whether on land, sea, or air."*

**STILL IN OUR "CIVVIES," WE RODE A BUS FROM** Phoenix to Long Beach, California, to Fort MacArthur. We stayed there until October 3. We were tested, given some shots and received our initial uniforms. It was there that the inevitable happened and 99.9 percent of us were assigned to the infantry. I never found out what it took to beat the cut and get anything else.

While at Fort MacArthur, I visited the Phillip Rees family (cousins). One trip to downtown Los Angles and I bought a gold Army ring that I still have and still wear after 72 years.

Another bus trip and on October 3 we arrived at Camp Roberts, California. This was an IRTC (Infantry Replacement Training Center). As we got off the bus the guys already there called out to us: "You'll be sorry." We were assigned to the 4th Platoon, D Company of the 95th Infantry Training Battalion. There were four squads of about 12 men in each platoon. We were scheduled to receive 15 weeks of infantry basic training.

First, I want to compare our training with the image, and probable reality, of Marine boot camp. To my knowledge and experience no effort was made to break our wills and remold us into the official pattern. Unlike the typical "DI" (drill instructor), our leaders were not in-your-face sadistic "monsters." They told us that over 90% of us would see combat. When (not if) we did, 10% of us would be killed, 25% would be wounded and 15% would be injured or have battle fatigue. This meant we would have a 50/50 chance of returning unscathed. Therefore, their job and ours was to do all we could to prepare us for infantry combat and to try and beat the odds on the casualties. It was a hard, strenuous and busy 15 weeks, but my memories of them are more positive than negative.

Some of the objectives that I observed include:

1. Developing physical strength, endurance and good health.
2. Developing discipline and team work.
3. Learning military skills and weapons proficiency.
4. Personal care and survival.
5. Lower-level tactics.
6. Psychological preparation and indoctrination.

I think they did a pretty good job in achieving these objectives. Early in the war they couldn't do this, but by the time we were there (late 1944), they could have brought more combat-experienced veterans into the training cadre and taught less theory and more direct battle savvy.

Next, I want to get the "greasy kid stuff" out of the way. I was never convinced that all the close order drilling, formations and parades, inspections and the perpetuation of many Army traditions, myths and customs really related to or prepared us for combat. Calisthenics, while not always popular, were a necessary evil for building strength and endurance, as were long marches with full field packs. The training was strenuous, often started early and ended late—with some sleep deprivation—but was nothing compared to combat.

## Weapons Training

The M-1 Garand Rifle was our one basic, primary weapon. We quickly learned that it was not a "gun" and to always call it a "rifle." We had our own assigned rifle to keep track of and to keep clean and in good working order. Therefore, we memorized the serial numbers of our rifle. We learned to take it apart and clean and re-assemble it blind folded.

The Garand, when loaded, weighed right at 10 pounds. Besides the leather sling, it had 3 wood parts and 58 steel parts. We spent many hours on the firing range (both shooting and manning the targets) until we developed a degree of skill. I qualified for the sharpshooter level and held the MOS (Military Operations Specialty) of 745, Rifleman.

The BAR, the Browning Automatic Rifle, was similar to the M-1 but was fully automatic.

The carbine was a smaller, lighter rifle that used 30-caliber ammunition but smaller bullets and had less accuracy, shorter range and less "stopping power." It was used mainly by officers, tankers, flame thrower men and radio operators.

The 30-caliber, air-cooled machine gun was a real work horse in the infantry company.

The 60mm mortar was another staple that I liked working with. It involved more team work.

The 45-caliber M1911 pistol was used some but like the carbine was limited.

The bazooka was a very effective rocket but had a limited range.

Hand and rifle grenades were an essential part of the infantryman's arsenal and were fun but dangerous to use.

Mines, booby traps and demolitions.

The bayonet was a dreadful weapon on the front of our M-1 rifles. Bayonet training was my least enjoyable activity. I dreaded the thought of being in close enough contact with the enemy to actually use the bayonet, and I thank God that I never had to.

## CLOTHING AND EQUIPMENT

Our basic training attire was fatigues and field jackets. We wore high-top shoes and lace leggings. We had two pairs of shoes (with "x" and "o" on the instep) and wore each pair on alternate days. We mostly wore plastic helmet liners and later gradually adjusted to adding the steel "pots." Besides our rifles and bayonets we wore our ammunition belt, canteen, first aid kit, back pack with one blanket and one-half of a pup tent, entrenching tool and a gas mask. All socks and shirts, towels, underwear and handkerchiefs had to be brown and not white. This served two purposes: (1) to be less visible to the enemy and (2) to be less obvious when they were filthy dirty. We could not have any jewelry except a wrist watch, which should be in a pocket or covered by a sleeve. Our dog tags were to be kept inside our shirt.

The one glaring problem (for me, at least) was having to wear eyeglasses. The nickel-framed GI glasses and glass lenses were obviously a highly reflective item. The only consolation was that the Japanese, as a people, were chronically myopic (near sighted), and more of them wore glasses than the Americans.

Other activities included learning to use our gas masks, learning about different gases that might be used and having both planned and surprise, random gas drills. We had several obstacle courses and simulated battle ranges with live ammunition. Also, we had landing net practices—the

HOLLY WITH M-1 RIFLE AT CAMP ROBERTS, CALIFORNIA, 1944

basic rule was to *always* hold the vertical ropes and not the horizontal so no one could step on your fingers. KP, or Kitchen Police, was always the subject of jokes. Actually, it was often easier than the training that you got out of to do KP. Peeling potatoes was ridiculed, but it was a sitting down job and no big deal. Washing trays and pots and pans was a hot steamy standing job and not my favorite. I watched the food being delivered to the mess hall and it looked normal. I always marveled at how the Army could louse it up and understood why they called them "mess" halls. A favorite cartoon was of a soldier sitting out by the garbage cans eating away. The cook comes out and says, "What makes you think you're any better than anyone else? Get back in the mess hall with everyone else."

We were exposed to the PX (Post Exchange) and the chapel (Protestant, Catholic or Jewish). Our barracks were two-story frame buildings with a latrine on the first floor. We had double-deck steel cots and spent a lot of time sweeping, scrubbing and standing inspection, both scheduled (every Saturday morning) and surprise. We had no privacy in the latrines, which had rows of lavatories, commodes and a large group shower. Outside the shower was a large low flat pan with an antiseptic solution that you had to walk through after your shower. This was to prevent athlete's foot or any other problem. One of the "pachucos" was on latrine duty, and he "reasoned" that if one cup of the chemical was good then two was better and three even better. It was so strong it was eating the skin off our feet. It reinforced the adage to not think—just do it the Army way.

No dissertation about the Army would be complete without mention the infamous "short arms inspection." On mild days we stripped down to our shoes, put on our raincoats and stood outside in long lines to undergo the ordeal. When it was cold we wore our overcoats.

After standing in line, outside, you filed into a building, hiked up your raincoat or overcoat and were told to "bend over and spread your cheeks." After this detailed perusal of your posterior anatomy you turned around and were told to "skin it back and milk it down." Presumably the inspectors were doctors and they were looking for symptoms of sexually transmitted diseases. Many of the soldiers had been circumcised and many had not. Even after a number of these "short arms inspections" they were always embarrassing and degrading to me.

Equally memorable are the vivid recollections of the incomparable GI "VD" movies. Few things could have been as persuasive as these in steering one to a celibate life in a monastery. The gruesome images of the ravages of the male and female bodies from venereal diseases were designed to put the fear of God in all us GI's.

Of less impact were the indoctrination films that sought to remind us that we were at war with Japan, Germany and Italy. Their goal was to whet our appetites to make us want to go forth and kill every one of them. This made it easier to evade the moral dilemma involved with the massive killing of war, whether on land, sea, or air.

Another important activity was digging foxholes, which was more physical than mental. This was good training for us since this was a daily activity in combat. Of course, the nature of the soil was a factor (on Okinawa we couldn't always dig down in the coral and had to build above ground protection) and in training we tended to dig too shallow and under fire we tended to dig too deep. Rain and ground water could be a factor, and loose soil could lead to a cave-in—not good. The ultimate test was to be taken to a field and told to "dig in" because tanks would be coming in so many minutes to ride over our positions. This was excellent motivation, and we quickly and effectively dug our holes and survived the tank pass over.

## Peripheral Activities

Some of the older, more mature trainees were picked to be acting squad leaders. I was picked to be an assistant squad leader. We were all BAPs, and it carried no rank but was added work and carried some prestige. One of the other squad leaders was a nationally known and published cartoonist named Virgil I. Partch, who signed all his cartoons "VIP." He did a "portrait" of me one time when we came in from a march, which I still have.

During basic training at Camp Roberts, I spent several weekend passes going to the Los Angeles area to visit my parents, who had moved to Van Nuys and North Hollywood. On one of these trips my brother Gil was there on leave, and a snapshot of us was taken. It is shown on the title page of this book.

We were given the opportunity to apply for Infantry Officer Candidate School (OCS). I took the written exam and apparently did quite well. This was followed by a series of interviews that were interesting and challenging, but I breezed through them, too. I guess there was an assumption that if we were in the infantry we were physically fit for OCS. After completion

Holly's Trainee Portrait by "Partch"

of basic training, those of us who passed the exam and interviews were detained and on orders for transfer to Fort Benning, Georgia. The final step was a physical exam, and I passed everything but the eye test. With glasses I could see 20/20, but without glasses I couldn't see the minimum 20/100 required. So I was "redlined" and resumed the inevitable move to

4TH PLATOON, D COMPANY,
95TH INFANTRY TRAINING BATTALION, JAN. 1944

war. At first I was disappointed that I didn't make OCS and become a "shavetail, Second Looie, 90-day wonder" Later I came to realize that if I had, I would have missed combat in World War II and would have done occupation duty, and almost inevitably been a platoon leader in Korea.

About the middle of December 1944 the Battle of the Bulge occurred in Europe. In the crisis that followed they pulled the battalion that had 14 weeks of basic training and sent them to the East Coast and on to France. Days later they pulled the 13th week, then the 12th and finally the 11th! We had by then completed 10 weeks and had one foot on a banana peel. I knew and knew of guys who left Camp Roberts who flew to France, fought and were wounded, and were back in England within seven days. I would like to have gone to Europe but not under those circumstances and without adequate training. Once again I was back on track for the Asiatic Pacific Theater of Operations.

The people in basic training were a motley crew. D Company commander was a 1st Lieutenant and the 4th Platoon leader was a 2nd Lieutenant and neither of them had any combat experiences. We had two sergeants (one of which had been in combat) and two corporals in the cadre. The trainees were mostly 18-19 years old, but there was a sprinkling of "older men" even in their 30s. Most were white, but many were Mexican. We even had a few Indians (Native Americans) and one "India Indian."

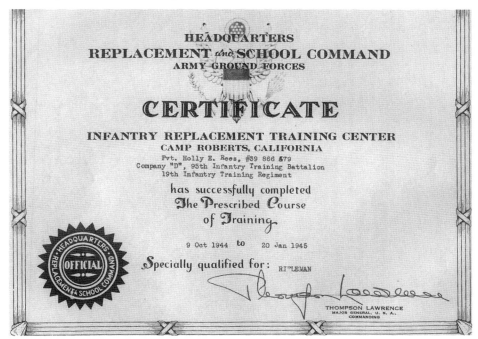

TRAINING CERTIFICATE, IRTC CAMP ROBERTS

Most were high school graduates or less, but a few were better educated. Most were poor working class, but some (like Virgil Partch) were better off. We didn't bond as much in basic training as we did later in our "permanent" assignment and in combat. Included is a graduation picture of the 4th Platoon, D Company, 95th Infantry Training Battalion.

All in all, I think our 15 weeks of basic training was adequate and prepared us for the rigor and challenges of infantry combat.

Ships unloading supplies at one of the many landing points on Okinawa (U.S. Navy)

# 4

## Leave & Route to Okinawa

*"We saw destroyers and destroyer escorts, battleships, aircraft carriers, troop ships, tankers, hospital ships, ammunition ships, and mostly cargo ships. For this country boy from land-locked Arizona, I was blown away by this vast armada, which was by far the largest in the Pacific and rivaled the D-Day Normandy invasion in scope."*

I LEFT CAMP ROBERTS ON FEBRUARY 4 AND had a delay-in-route to visit Prescott and North Hollywood before reporting to Fort ORD, California, on February 21. Before leaving Camp Roberts I celebrated my 19th birthday on January 21.

Fort ORD was the only military installation I know of that is not named for a person. It stands for "Overseas Replacement Depot," thus the ORD. While there we were asked if we could swim 50 yards, and I doubted that I could and said so. Each evening I had to go to swimming lessons after completing the day's activities (marching, rifle range, etc.). I hoped I would flunk and *not* get to go overseas. Without ever swimming 50 yards, our time was up and we moved on. A memory of Fort ORD was the recreation center that sold a pitcher (large) of Pabst Blue Ribbon beer for 50 cents and snacks for practically nothing. We would sometimes skip supper in the mess hall and go to the rec hall for a liquid diet. On March 7 we boarded a troop train for Seattle, Washington.

We were in Pullman cars that were designed for two in a lower berth and one in the upper. The Army did them one better and put three in the lower and two in the upper.

We learned to take turns sleeping rather than crowd in like sardines. The food on the troop train wasn't too good either!

Because we were heading for the "South Pacific," they took our woolen clothes away from us, and we had only khakis and fatigues and field jackets. We were issued our combat boots, which we liked better than canvas leggings. Also, they were a status symbol for the combat infantry.

After surviving the troop train, we then spent March 9-22 at Fort Lewis, Washington. The barracks were ancient, drafty and cold. The weather was damp and cold, and without our woolens we were miserable. More practice, shots, paperwork, etc. and we were ready to go to war. We were trucked to the Port of Embarkation in Seattle and boarded the *SS Aquaprince*, a troop ship. If you wore a shoe size smaller than an 8 or larger than a 12, you had to carry on an extra pair of combat boots because they might not be available later. One guy wore a 14 and had to have an extra barracks bag to carry his extra boots. We also had to constantly keep our gas masks handy and were docked if we lost them. This later appeared ridiculous since one of the first things we did when assigned to the Seventh Infantry Division was to throw our gas masks on a big pile where they added gasoline and burned them. Others could steal or exchange gas masks, but mine had prescription eyeglasses in them.

The weather was very stormy and the sea rough after we left Seattle and Puget Sound. Nearly everyone was seasick. I think I might have made it past the motion, but when everyone around you was gagging and vomiting, the noise and smell was too much and I joined them at the rail. I actually got sick and went to the sick bay and was diagnosed with "cat fever."

While in sick bay, there were a number of wounded veterans from the 442nd Regimental Combat Team (the Nisei, the most decorated regiment in the World War II Army) on their way home to Hawaii.

On March 31 we landed right by the clock tower in downtown Honolulu. After a short trip on trucks we loaded on a narrow-gauge railroad to head inland. It was used for hauling pineapples and sugar cane but had been commandeered by the Army to haul troops. Anyway, we got nearly to Wahiawa and the going was too steep for the engine to handle—so we got off and pushed the train over the crest and went on. I have pushed many a car in my 90 years, but this was the only time I pushed a train.

We stayed at the Army Ground Forces Replacement Depot #13 from March 31 until April 7. We did mostly calisthenics and marching. We had a formation early every afternoon, and they said that it rained every day at 2 p.m. It could be blue skies and sunshine at 1 pm., and sure enough it would cloud up and rain at 2 p.m. (on our formation) and then clear up again. I remember how red the soil was there.

On April 7 we again loaded on the train (downhill this time) and went back to Honolulu. This time we boarded a larger troop ship, the *USS Bottineau*, for the 20-day convoy journey to Saipan, Marianas Islands.

Two incidents of note took place, which stood out in the boring, crowded transit. Many of the GIs played poker to relieve the boredom. One game I witnessed was played on the top of the berths by a large ventilation fan. One of the guys (probably distracted by a good hand) leaned back and his ear went through the grill and the fan blade sheared off part of his ear. Blood blew out all over everything, and he was escorted to sick bay. A short time later, well-bandaged and chastened, he returned and said: "Deal me in."

Another group, intent on coping with the boredom, pulled off a hatch and went below in a cargo area. They found lots of cases of tins of fine chocolate for the officers, which they opened and passed topside for the enjoyment of the GIs on the ship. Security was tight on the convoy, but you could have traced our path across the Central Pacific by following the floating chocolate tins (sans chocolate). When the captain learned of this tragic event, he was furious and going to court martial everyone involved. When he asked for the guilty ones to step forward, every GI in earshot stepped forward. (Most everyone had enjoyed the chocolate even though only a few brought them out.) Obviously he had to deliver a troop ship load of infantry replacements and the matter was dropped.

We ate all of our meals standing up and usually had navy beans for breakfast. We tried to do calisthenics on the crowded ship. I enjoyed topside (the sleeping berths were hot, smoky, smelly and crowded), especially standing at the rail and watching the ocean (and tins) flow by. We passed by Eniwetok in the Marshalls but did not go ashore. Finally on April 27 we landed on Saipan in the Marianas Islands.

We spent five days on Saipan at the AGF Replacement Depot #23 mainly to stretch our legs and get some exercise and relief. This was our first contact with real estate that had been taken from the Japs the year before.

Before reaching Saipan we crossed the 180th Meridian, and the sailors would like to have harassed us, for the usual ceremony. They were totally outnumbered, and we were in no mood for such greasy kid stuff.

Sailors and travelers have two main ceremonies to observe. The first is crossing the equator and the second is crossing the 180th Meridian, also known as the International Date Line.

The ones who have done this before conduct the initiation for the new crossers. Some of this can be good clean fun and a relief from boredom at sea. It can degrade into some real hazing, however. I suspect that the ratio of old hands to neophytes plays a big part in how the initiation progresses. In our case the number of Army troops far outnumbered the Navy personnel.

On May 1 we boarded the APA 235, which was an assault troop ship, and by May 4th we had reached Okinawa in the Ryukyu Islands. The battle there had begun with the landing on Easter Sunday, April 1. On this last leg of our journey to Okinawa, the rumor was rampant that Okinawa was literally crawling with poisonous snakes. I was on Okinawa for 43 days, and I never saw a snake!

The only other topic of note is my reaction to the hundreds of ships we saw and passed as we got closer and closer and finally disembarked. It began as we passed the picket line some 125 miles offshore. These were the eyes and ears of the Navy to spot kamikaze planes and to help protect the fleet. We saw destroyers and destroyer escorts, battleships, aircraft carriers, troop ships, tankers, hospital ships, ammunition ships and mostly cargo ships. For this country boy from land-locked Arizona, I was blown away by this vast armada, which was by far the largest in the Pacific and rivaled the D-Day Normandy invasion in scope.

The armada was assembled from 11 different ports, from as far as Seattle (6,000 miles) to Leyte and many other locations. A total of 1,457 ships were involved: 318 combat ships and 1,139 auxiliary ships. There were 40 aircraft carriers, 18 battleships, 200 destroyers, 60 miscellaneous ships, 430 assault transports and landing ships and the rest were cargo, tanker, hospital or other categories.

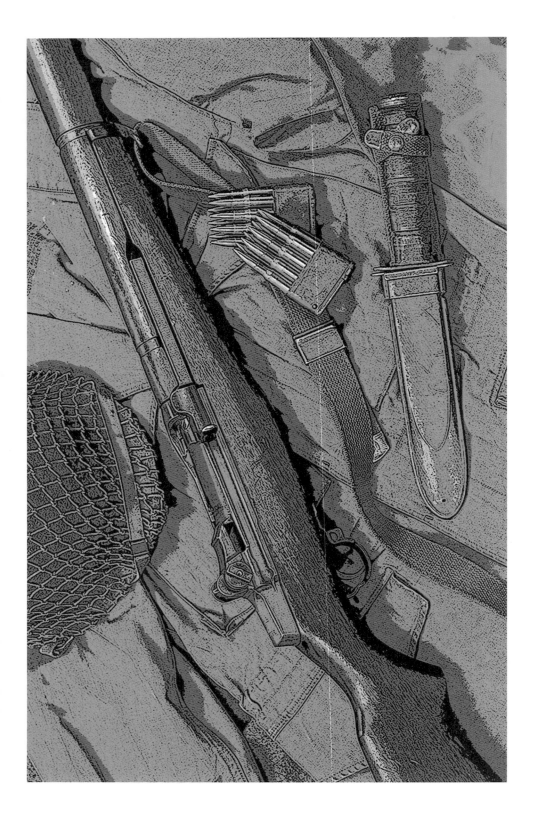

# 5

## Infantry Company Weapons & Equipment

### A Listing and Comparison

*"Probably the biggest difference was their weakness as an organization. They had a much tighter pecking order and caste system. Each person was probably well-trained and proficient in his area of expertise. However, they neglected cross-training and flexibility."*

**I CAN'T RECALL READING IN ANY OF THE BOOKS** on Okinawa a listing or comparison of weapons. A few references apply to an isolated item. This information may not be worth much to the declining number of veterans, but to the less well-informed civilian, references to the standard arms we used, such as an M1 or BAR, might prove valuable. So, before relating my combat experiences, I have included this chapter on weapons and equipment we carried.

Both the GIs and the Japanese were good soldiers, well-trained and equipped. The GIs had more and better equipment and superior fire power. The Japanese often had pre-training such as military school, ROTC type, etc., whereas we were mainly citizen soldiers. They might have had the edge on motivation—to serve and die for the emperor. Both sides emphasized physical conditioning, and I think we were both "lean and mean."

Probably the biggest difference was their weakness as an organization. They had a much tighter pecking order and caste system. Each person was probably well-trained and proficient in his area of expertise. However, they neglected cross-training and flexibility. If we had a mortar man killed or wounded, a rifleman could step in and fill the breach thanks to our basic training. This was true of most of our functions. Also, we often brought in replacements (I was one of them), and they could be assimilated and productive in short order.

This problem was even more pronounced between the troops and the non-commissioned officers and the officers. If one was killed or seriously wounded, the others were lost and incapable of adjusting and reorganizing. We had much talent, and a private could take over the squad, the sergeant the platoon, the lieutenant the company.

## Infantry Rifles

The shoulder-fired rifle was the basic essential weapon for both the Japanese and us. Nearly every U.S. infantryman was armed with an M1 "Garand" rifle. With one .30-06 cal. round in the chamber and a clip of eight inserted, the M1 (with carrying strap) weighed right at 10 pounds. It was a gas-operated semi-automatic weapon. It was rugged, dependable, and formidable. It had a good range and was reasonably accurate.

For snipers and special uses, we often used (with a scope) the 1903 Springfield or 1916 Enfield rifles. These were both bolt-action magazine-fed rifles, no match for the clip-fed semi-automatic M1 in direct combat.

We also used a .30 cal. carbine that was shorter, lighter and fired a smaller size and weight of bullet. It was no match for the M1 but was usedful where size and weight were a factor, particularly for radiomen, transport troops, and officers who were not leading troops in direct combat.

Each infantryman wore an ammunition belt that held 10 clips, each with eight bullets, and often added one or more bandoliers of additional ammunition. Thus, each soldier carried nine rounds at hand and a reserve arsenal of 80-150 more. The M1, Springfield, Enfield, Browning Automatic Rifle, and the air-cooled machine guns all fired the same .30-06 cal. rounds.

The Japanese Imperial Army infantry on Okinawa used two different rifles, the older .25 cal. (6.5mm) Arisaka and the newer .31 cal. (7.7mm) Arisaka. Both were "mauser type" internal magazine bolt-action rifles.

Both were quite accurate, but they had several disadvantages: (1) being bolt-action vs. our semi-automatics, (2) having two sizes of ammunition that were not interchangeable and (3) the .25 cal. (6.5mm) was too light to be an effective combat weapon. The Japanese also had a carbine version, but I never saw one.

## M-1 Garand (U.S. Rifle caliber .30-06, M-1)
semi-automatic chambered for .30-06 Springfield rifle cartridge
(Armémuseum)

## M1903 Springfield (u.s. Rifle Cal. .30-06, Model 1903)
Bolt Action chambered for .30-06 Springfield rifle cartridge
(Armémuseum)

## M-1 Carbine (U.S. Carbine, Caliber .30, M1)
semi-automatic chambered for .30 cal. (7.62mm) cartridge
(Armémuseum)

## Arisaka Type 38 Rifle (Imperial Japanese Army)
Bolt Action chambered for 6.5mm cartridge
(Armémuseum)

## Arisaka Type 99 Rifle (Imperial Japanese Army)
Bolt Action chambered for 7.7mm cartridge
(Armémuseum)

## Specialized Automatic Weapons

Also called the "grease gun," the Thompson sub-machine gun was a short, stubby, fully automatic carbine-style machine gun. It fired the .45 cal. ACP round, the cartridge created for the 1911 model Colt semi-automatic sidearm. It was mainly shorter range and very effective in close combat but no match for the M1 Garand, the Browning Automatic Rifle or the .30 cal. machine gun at medium and longer range.

Thompson Sub-Machine Gun
Automatic Fire chambered for .45 cal. ACP cartridge
(Armémuseum)

The American Browning Automatic Rifle (BAR) was similar to the M1 but was select fire—it could fire single shots or in fully automatic mode, like a machine gun. It also weighed about twice as much as an M1. It used the same 30-06 cal. ammunition fed from a 20-round magazine. Besides being shoulder fired, it had two bipod legs for prone position stability. When supported by a sling, it could be fired even from the hip. to provide "walking fire." I am not aware of the Japanese having an equivalent weapon to our BAR, which was a mainstay in our arsenal of weapons.

Browning Automatic Rifle (BAR M1918)
Select Fire chambered for .30-06 Springfield rifle cartridge
(U.S. Army Heritage Museum)

# Machine Guns

## M1919A4 Browning Medium Machine Gun
### Automatic Fire chambered for .30-06 Springfield rifle cartridge
(U.S. Army Heritage Museum)

In the rifle company we used 30-caliber, light air-cooled machine guns. They used a cloth belt to feed the bullets. We usually used a three-man team: the gunner with the machine gun itself, the assistant gunner with the base and a third man to provide ammunition. This also was a mainstay in our combat capability.

## Japanese Type 96 Light Machine Gun
### Automatic Fire chambered for 6.5x50mm Arisaka cartridge
(U.S. Army)

The Japanese had several different machine guns, and all were effective and deadly. A difference between rifles and machine guns was that, in addition to regular bullets, the machine guns fired every fifth round a "tracer" that could be seen and helped in aiming the weapon. Another key difference was that Japanese machine guns were rapid fire and ours were slower firing. The rapid fire used and wasted ammunition and were harder to keep supplied. We also had armor-piercing bullets for special use.

## Sidearms

PISTOLS: Unlike Gen. Patton, who was famous for his cowboy-style pearl-handled revolvers, we carried the M1911 .45 cal. semi-automatic pistol. Infantry riflemen didn't use them very much in combat, but they were light, portable and packed a punch in close range combat.

### M1911A1 Semi-automatic Pistol
#### chambered for .45 cal. Colt ACP cartridge
(Armémuseum)

The Japanese Nambu semi-automatic pistols and revolvers were manufactured in several models that fired the 8mm or 9mm cartridge, and some models could be fitted with a shoulder stock.

### Japanese Nambu Pistol Model 14
#### chambered for .8x22 mm cartridge
(Armémuseum)

BAYONETS, KNIVES, SWORDS: We used a 10-inch bayonet that attached to the front of our rifles. These were for very close combat, and I am eternally grateful that I never had to use mine. (Actually very few soldiers had to.) We were not issued sheath knives, but many GIs had their own. My uncle, Silas Holly, made me a beauty that I carried in combat.

## U.S. M1 Bayonet — 3 Point Types (U.S. Army)

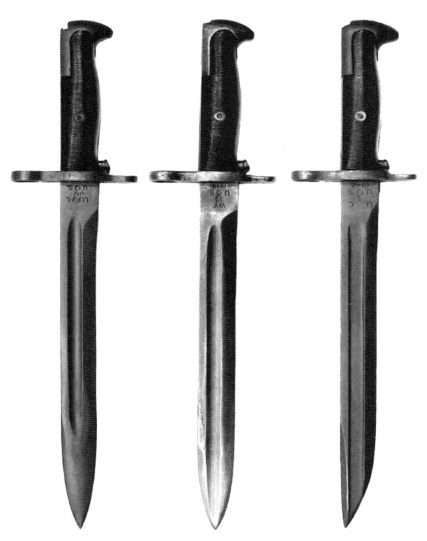

The Japanese infantry riflemen used a 16-inch bayonet with a hook at the base.

### Type 30 Japanese Bayonet
(Armémuseum)

The Japanese officers had Samurai (Shin Gunto) type swords that were more ceremonial badges of rank and status than utilitarian weapons. G.I.s prized them as souvenirs, and I always regretted that I never got one.

### Type 98 shin guntō
Imperial Japanese Army "new Military" sword
(Armémuseum)

# Squad-Portable Ordnance

MORTARS: The 60mm mortar was a high-trajectory weapon that we had at hand in the rifle company. Larger mortars could be called on for help, but "our own" 60mms were good for both offense and defense and readily available.

M2 60 MM MORTAR
FIRES 3 LB. 60MM (2.36") SHELL, 18 ROUNDS PER MINUTE
(U.S. ARMY HERITAGE MUSEUM)

    Mortar teams consisted of a three-man operations crew and a fourth man as a spotter. The mortar man carried the tube and legs, the assistant carried the base plate, and the third carried the ammunition. Rarely could they see their targets so they needed a spotter to guide them. They used mostly "HE" or high-explosive shells but also had "WP" or white-phosphorus to see and provide smoke. Our heavy weapons company had 81mm mortars and battalion had 4.2-inch chemical mortars.

The Japanese had 50-, 70-, and 81mm mortars that were similar to ours. They also had a small, one-man "knee mortar" that was more like a grenade launcher. They were light, mobile, very effective and deadly.

### JAPANESE TYPE 89 GRENADE DISCHARGER (KNEE MORTAR)
#### FIRES 28 OZ. 50MM (1.97") ROUND (U.S. ARMY)

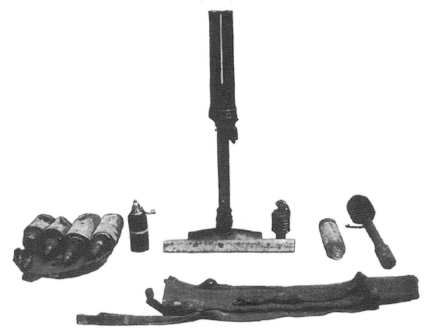

GRENADES: Both the Japanese and the U.S. had several different kinds of hand grenades. They were very effective and deadly but limited by their weight and the distance they could be thrown. Timing was crucial since they could be thrown back, roll downhill, etc. We had many casualties from shrapnel from our own grenades, as well as from the Japanese grenades.

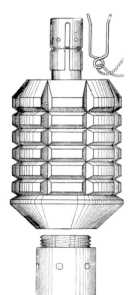

### JAPANESE TYPE 10
#### FRAGMENTATION GRENADE
#### 50 GRAMS EXPLOSIVE, 7-SECOND DELAY
(U.S. ARMY)

### U.S. Army MKII
#### Fragmentation Grenade
2 oz. explosive, 5-second delay
(U.S. Army)

We both had "rifle grenades" that could be launched by a rifle that increased the range and accuracy. The recoil of these was tremendous, and consequently they were not used very often.

### M7 grenade launcher with 22 mm grenade
fitted on the end of an M1 Garand rifle
(U.S. Army photo

FLAME THROWER: The flame thrower was another highly effective niche weapon (one that I hated being near).

They consisted of heavy and awkward tanks of napalm (jellied aviation gasoline) on a back pack with a hand-held and hand-aimed hose and nozzle. The range was short, but the stream of fire was deadly, especially if you could get it into a bunker. A much better weapon was a tank-mounted flame thrower that had more quantity and longer range plus the tank's armor for protection.

The flame thrower operators had a short life expectancy and were some of the bravest soldiers I saw. They also needed riflemen to cover them as a team effort.

## M1A1 FLAMETHROWER
FLAMETHROWER TEAM ATTACKING JAPANESE BUNKER (U.S. CHEMICAL WARFARE SERVICE)

BAZOOKA: This was a shoulder-fired rocket that was used mainly for anti-tank and bunker use. They were about 2.5 inches in diameter and about 5 feet long. They had their niche but lacked range and required a blast zone behind them when fired. The bazooka man was very vulnerable and usually had a group of riflemen covering him.

## M1 Rocket Launcher (Bazooka)
### (Smithsonian Institute)

DEMOLITIONS: We had explosives to blow up bridges, bunkers, etc. and to make satchel charges. Also, mines and "Bangalore" torpedoes were used for clearing barbed wire and mines.

SATCHEL CHARGE (U.S. ARMY)

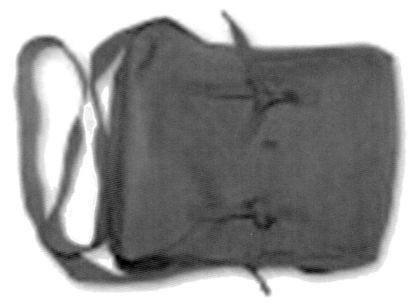

"BANGALORE" TORPEDO (U.S. ARMY PHOTO)

## Communications

We had one SCR-300 radio in the company to communicate with battalion, air support, artillery and JASCO (Joint Assault Signal Company). It was a backpack that weighed about 45 pounds and was a favorite target for Japanese snipers and infiltrators.

SCR-300 BATTERY-POWERED FM VOICE RECEIVER TRANSMITTER
(NATIONAL ELECTRONICS MUSEUM)

We had about a half dozen SCR 536 radios for communication between company and platoons and between platoons. Those were small hand-held radios and weighed about five pounds. We had sound power telephones that could be used for battalion to company and intra-company use. We also used the telephone wire to physically communicate silently at night. I often strung the telephone wire out in the evening between foxholes on the front line with accompanying sniper harassment. Each CO had one or two "runners" or messengers to carry orders if the radios or telephones were out. This could be a dangerous job—one that got me a Bronze Star! (explained later)

### SCR-536 "WALKIE-TALKIE) RECEIVER TRANSMITTER
#### (U.S. ARMY ILLUSTRATION)

We usually had an artillery captain with us who served as spotter and liaison. He had a soldier with him to carry an SCR 300, which he used with the battery supporting us.

## OTHER EQUIPMENT

BARBED WIRE: Especially at night and when we were holding a fixed position (which we rarely did), we had concertina and barbed wire to put out in front of the lines to deter Japanese infiltration.

OPTICS/NAVIGATION: Most officers had binoculars, compasses, watches and maps, but few, if any, enlisted men did. Some acquired items from wounded officers and/or scrounged them from the Japanese. The Japanese binoculars were of good quality and made good souvenirs.

LUMINOUS PANELS: We carried a number of orange oil cloth panels, each about 1.5 feet x 5-6 feet long that were kept rolled up in the canvas bags. For air strikes and artillery we would "mark" the front line by rolling out these panels in front of us (I'll relate an example later when this did not work).

# TRANSPORTATION

We had one jeep in each infantry company for multiple uses: to haul food, water and ammunition up and carry the wounded back. Because of the incessant rain and mud, ours was often unusable as well as being a tempting target for enemy artillery.

U.S. ARMY WILLYS MA3 JEEP JUNE 1942
(UNITED STATES LIBRARY OF CONGRESS'S PRINTS AND PHOTOGRAPHS DIVISION)

# MEDICAL SERVICE

This listing would not be complete without including and praising the combat medics. We had two assigned to our company, who carried no weapons and wore a Red Cross armband. They were two of the bravest and best—Glick and Waldowski. Their job was to get to the wounded ASAP and provide field first aid. Often at the risk of their own lives, they would apply tourniquets, use sulfa and bandage wounds, give morphine if appropriate and assist the wounded back to safety for more advanced and complete treatment. Often our riflemen would assist in the carrying or dragging of the wounded back. Sometimes we would have to wait for a lull or break or nightfall to retrieve the wounded. We often had to leave the dead, and after we moved on Graves Registration personnel would take over. All of our dead were buried in the 7th Infantry Division Cemetery on Okinawa and were later re-interred to the Punchbowl on Oahu.

### MEDICAL EVACUATION BY STRETCHER ON OKINAWA
TRANSPORT OF THE WOUNDED DURING COMBAT USUALLY REQUIRED THAT THEY BE CARRIED PART OF THE WAY BY STRETCHER TO MEET AMBULANCE JEEPS.

(U.S. PHOTO)

## What an Infantryman Carried ...

I have mentioned weight on a number of the weapons because that was a perennial problem for the GI. We were loaded down with stuff, and it was always a problem of balance to weigh with essential, necessities and optional items (such as souvenirs and number of hand grenades, amount of rations and amount of ammo to carry). This was hard for the rifleman, but even more a problem for the SCR 300 radioman, mortar men, flame thrower men, machine gun crews, etc. We often carried 60-70 pounds, and this limited maneuverability, flexibility and stamina.

### Infantry squad on Okinawa
Browning Automatic rifle, M1 Garand, Flamethrower, SSCR-300 Radio, Full packs, canteens, sidearms, entrenching tools, Shelter sections. ammunition, rations.

(U.S. Army photo)

Most infantrymen, in addition to their weapons, hand grenades and ammunition carried the following:

A. Entrenching tool—small pick and shovel to dig foxholes, an essential survival.

B. Canteen—sometimes two and often the only water we had for the day.

C. Mess kit and rations—in combat usually only C or K rations. If we got relieved we might get "10 in one" rations.

D. First aid kit

E. Bayonet

F. Pack with change of underwear, socks, stationery, souvenirs, a field jacket, a blanket, a poncho and half a pup tent. I can't emphasize it enough, we were loaded down.

CLOTHING: We wore fatigues with no insignia, steel helmets, ammunition belt and combat boots. The Japanese were similar but wore a sort of tennis shoe like a mitten. The tobi had the big toe separate from the other toes. This left a visible track but was good for night infiltration. They were more like a tennis shoe and not as big, heavy and bulky as our combat boots.

# ORGANIZATION

I have tried to give a fairly exhaustive listing of the infantry company weapons and equipment. This could go on and on with pictures, specifications, instructions, etc., but I wanted a brief overview. Some of the other help we had from levels above the infantry rifle company included (and we were grateful for their help):

A. Heavy weapon company

B. Field artillery

C. Armored units/tanks

D. Transportation

E. Air support—land, naval

F. Naval guns and flares

G. Medical corps

H. Signal corps

I. Supply

J. Engineers and Seabees

K. Intelligence and cartography

The overall organization on Okinawa was the 10th Army commanded by Gen. Simon Bolivar Buckner. (We gave him an additional name, Oliver, so his initials would be SOB Buckner.) Under him were two corps, the Marine Corps, III Amphibious Corps and the 24th Army Corps. The Marines included the 1st, 5th and 6th Marine Divisions. Since much has been written about them, I won't include them in my comments. The 24th Army Corps under General John R. Hodge consisted of the 7th, 77th and 96th Infantry Divisions with the 27th Infantry Division attached.

The 7th Infantry Division was commanded by General Archibald V. Arnold and was made up of the 17th and 32nd Infantry Regiments, which were both regular Army regiments. Also the 184th Infantry Regiment,

## Lt. General Simon Bolivar Buckner

The last photograph of Lt. Gen. Buckner before he was killed during the closing days of the Battle of Okinawa by enemy artillery fire. (U.S. Army)

which was a California National Guard unit that had been called up for "the duration and six." The 184th Infantry Regiment was commanded by Colonel Roy A. Green. After the war the 184th was returned to the California National Guard, and the 31st Infantry Regiment replaced it in the 7th.

All infantry regiments (including the 184th) are made up of three battalions of infantry and other support units. The first battalion is made up of three rifle companies—A, B, C—and a heavy weapons company D. The second consists of companies E, F, G and has a heavy weapons company H. The third battalion includes rifle companies I, K and L and heavy weapons company M. We usually did not use the initials only but the Army jargon: Able, Baker, Charley, Dog, Easy, Fox, George, Harry, Item, King, Love and Mike. Our 3rd Battalion was commanded by Major James K. Bullock.

The rifle company commanded by a captain (our I Company was led by Capt. James W. Parker, from Eureka, California) consists of three rifle platoons, commanded by a second lieutenant, a weapons platoon and the company headquarters. Each platoon consists of three to four squads headed by a sergeant.

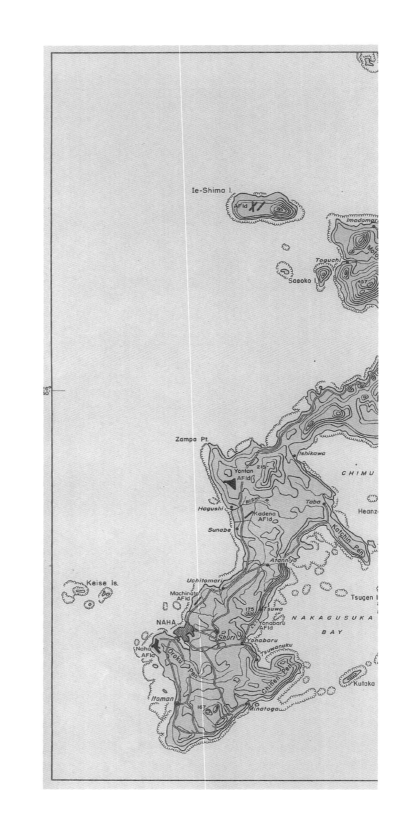

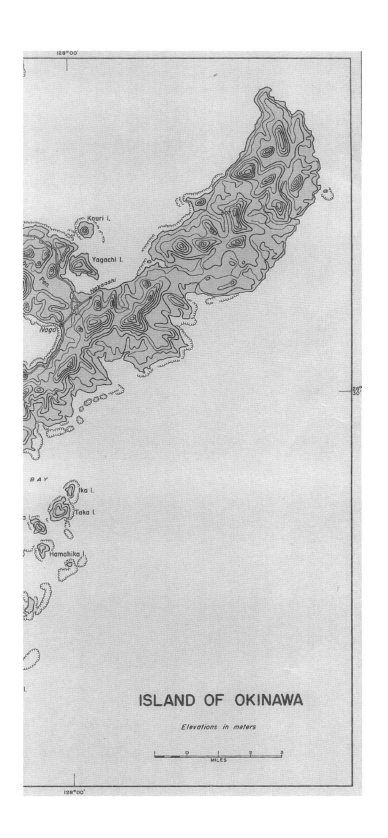

ISLAND OF OKINAWA

*Elevations in meters*

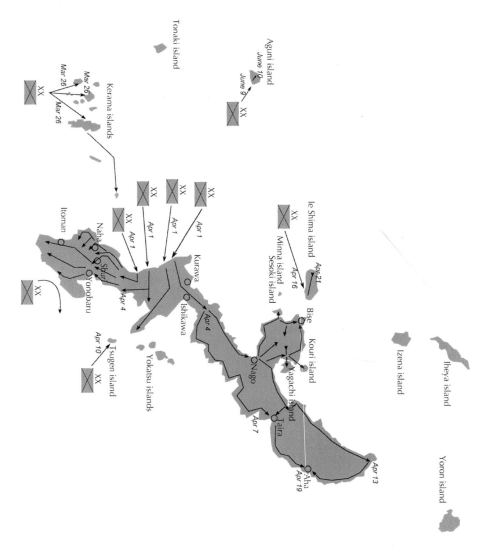

# Map of U.S. Operations on Okinawa
Originally from image:Okinawa.svg (GNU License)
Battle annotations taken from "Atlas of WWII" by John Keegan

# 6

## Combat on Okinawa

*"The CO stood just below the crest of Sugar Loaf Hill. With him were the 300 radioman, commo sergeant, and a messenger. Below them lay a peaceful pastoral scene. It had been worked by the Master's hand in the gentle greens of fertile hillsides, the browns of bare earth, the greys of the village of Keradera, and the mottled hues of a turbulent sky above. All too soon the red blood and bodies of the men of this command would rend the peaceful picture into the raging hell of a typical battlefield."*

**WE WENT DOWN THE LANDING NETS WITH** all our gear into Higgins boats for the trip to the shore. The harbor area was a mass of large, medium, and small boats unloading cargo. The shore was a mass (mess) of material piled up and waiting to be moved. We were taken by trucks to a vast hillside holding area.

As I was staggering along, lost in a vast crowd of several thousand replacements, someone yelled out, "Hey, Holly." This was one of the very few times in my life that my name was an advantage—there was obviously no other Holly in that crowd. I located Pvt. Gene Hayes. We spent the night together on the hillside, and the next day we received our assignments. He was to be in the 2nd Battalion, 184th Infantry Regiment, 7th Infantry Division, and I was to be in I company, 3rd Battalion.

The 7th Infantry Division had previously landed on and taken Attu and Kiska in the Aleution Islands, Kwajalein in the Marshals, and Leyte in the Philippines. Okinawa in the Ryukyus ws the 4th invasion made by the 7th ID.

Shortly afterward we were trucked to the area where the 7th Division was bivouacked, and we found our outfits. The 7th had been on the line for 40 days since making the initial landing on April 1st. The 40 days of combat were exhausting and depleting and the division was now in reserve for 10 days to rest and receive replacements.

The 7th had incurred 5,681 casualties during this first 40 days of combat. 636 were killed, 2,817 wounded, 16 missing, and 2,212 were non-enemy related (battle fatigue, illness, or injury). There were 1,691 of us replacements brought in to replace these casualties (to provide cannon fodder for the next phase), and 546 men returned to duty from hospitals.

We were able to get acquainted with the old timers and assimilate into our jobs before the 7th went back into combat. We later received a few replacements while on the line, and I am grateful to have had the chance to join the Division in reserve.

Gene Hayes and I were near each other and got together several times. Once Forest Bacus (also from the Prescott High School class of '44) who was already there, and in the 17th Regiment of the 7th Infantry Division, joined us.

During this time in reserve we had hot food and showers but slept on the ground in 2-man pup tents. (The monsoon rains hadn't started yet.) We saw several old movies in the evening and had time to write letters and relax. Things didn't seem all that plush to me then, but we would look back on them as the good old days.

We spent our time getting all our weapons and equipment ready for combat and discussing what was coming up and the later plans to attack the Japanese mainland in the fall.

I was paired up with Pfc. Don Kidd from Camillus, New York, and our job was to provide communication for the company—radio, telephone, and messenger. He was 21 (I was just 19) and a veteran of several battles with the 184th. He had been an NCO (non- commissioned officer) but had been busted for some reason. He was the company Casanova and probably received more mail than the rest of the company—from women in the states.

Don's favorite routine for the benefit of anyone listening, mostly strangers and newcomers, was for me to ask him if he had ever slept with a blonde. His reply was "Yes, many a time." Then, I would ask him if he had ever slept with a brunette, and he would reply, "Yes, many a time." Finally, I would ask him if had ever slept with a redhead and his answer was, "No—not a wink." His father was a doctor in Camillus. Don shaved nearly every day and trimmed his dapper mustache, scraped the mud off his fatigues, and formed a crease in the pants. He was probably the best-looking guy in the company, and you could see that he really was a ladies' man.

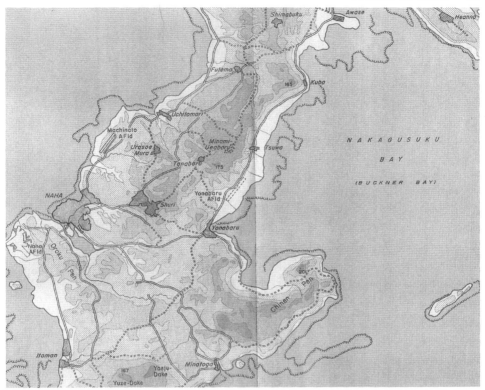

MAP OF SOUTHERN OKINAWA (U.S. ARMY
LOOKING SOUTH TO THE CONICAL HILL, BUCKNER BAY AND YANABARU

One time we received a replacement second lieutenant while on the line. He walked up to a small group of us (including Capt. Parker), faced Don and stuck out his hand to meet the CO. Don stuck out his hand. Just before connecting for a handshake, he swung his arm sideways, pointed to the captain and said he was the CO.

Our 10-day respite was soon over, and the 7th again headed back into combat. A very few of them had fought on Attu, Kwajalein, Leyte, and the first 40 days of Okinawa. Many had been added along the way, and a lot of us new replacements were heading into combat for the first time—our "baptism of fire."

After the initial landing, 40 days in combat, then 10 days in division reserve, the fought on for 32 more days until June 21st, when the U.S. command declared Okinawa secured.

Our first assignment was to pass by the east of Gaja, pass through the 96th ID between Nagagasuku Wan (later renamed Buckner Bay) and Conical Hill. This narrow coastal plain was the location of the town of Yonabaru, where I received my baptism of fire and later received a Bronze

ADVANCE ON SHURI (U.S. ARMY)

Star for action there. Yonabaru was the eastern end of the Naha-Shuri-Yonabaru defensive line. After taking and securing Yonabaru, we were to move south with some elements turning east to clear the Chinen Peninsula. Others headed west to go behind Conical Hill and behind the Japanese at Shuri to prevent their escape farther south. The main body just headed south. After we broke out of the narrow squeeze at Yonabaru, the 96th ID joined us on the eastern flank, and the Marines moved south on the western side.

During the next 32 days we advanced about 8 miles, which averaged ¼ of a mile a day. Of course, some days were a lot less, even zero, and some even more. If it had not been for the incessant rain and resulting mud, we could have been better supplied, had air cover and tank support, and accomplished our mission quicker, easier, and with fewer casualties.

On May 21st when I started combat, the front line extended from just north of Naha to north of Shuri and Conical Hill and ended just north of Yonabaru. This was a large crescent and was about 8,000 yards or 4½ to 5 miles long. The 1st and 5th Marine Divisions were on the west end, and the 96th and 7th Infantry Divisions were on the east.

Even though my recollections of the battle are crystal clear and vivid, even after nearly 71 years, I have been confirming and enhancing them with references. My main two references are: *Okinawa: The Last Battle* by Appleman et al. and *The Hourglass* by Love. For this first day, another excellent source is an article from Life Magazine that was dated June 18, 1944.

Life photographer/reporter W. Eugene Smith prepared an article on a typical 24-hour day in the life of a front line soldier. He, they, someone, picked Pfc. Terry Moore from F Company, 2nd Battalion, 184th Infantry, who was a BAR man. Gene Hayes was in the 2nd Battalion and I was in the 3rd. All of the information and pictures about taking Yonabaru were very close to where I was and almost mirror my experiences. It was so near, in fact, that I actually saw Smith taking pictures and thought he was crazy. Since he ended up wounded by shrapnel from a Japanese mortar shell, I still think he *was* crazy. In watching *The War* by Ken Burns on PBS, I saw two of the pictures from this article. Both said or implied that they were Marines and one was used on Peleliu and the other for Okinawa, but I knew they were the Army on Okinawa. Probably no one else would ever know the difference, and overall I thought *The War* was excellent.

We advanced up to the front in the pre-dawn darkness and attacked Yonabaru at first light. It was raining lightly and very muddy and miserable, not to mention the small arms fire and mortar fire from the Japanese.

There are a couple of topics I want to cover before we move on past the first day. This was one of the most memorable days in my life, but there are 31 more to go.

In the early afternoon of May 21st as we cleared Yonabaru and were moving up to the foothills to the south, I ran into Gene Hayes. He had a bullet hole in his helmet dead center and about ¾ of an inch below the top. The Japanese bullet had pierced the front, just grazed the top of his head, caught the back curvature, and went down and nicked him between the shoulder blades. A half an inch higher and it would have missed or bounced off, a half an inch lower and he would have been dead. He got his first Purple Heart on Day One. Several weeks later he was shot in the leg and evacuated.

In the other incident, we were stalled, and Capt. Parker wanted our company and the one next to us on the right to move out simultaneously. Our radios were wet and non-functioning, so he sent me as a runner to take a message to the CO of that company. He thought I'd have to go back, cross over, and then up to the CO. More through ignorance than bravery, I cut across (even part way behind some of the Japanese) and got the message delivered much sooner than he thought I would. Besides getting shot by the Japanese, I could easily have been shot by one of our trigger-happy soldiers. Capt. Parker was pleased, and both companies jumped off

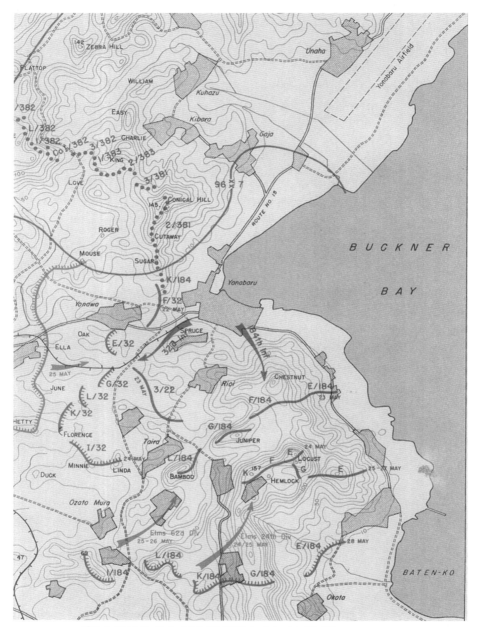

CLOSING IN ON SHURI, MAY 1945 (U.S. ARMY

together and moved on. Some 7 to 10 days later I was recommended for a Bronze Star Medal and it was turned down—as I was "just doing my job." Several years after the war someone was reviewing the battlefield reports and read the favorable comments Capt. Parker had written about me and on January 15, 1948, I was awarded the Bronze Star Medal. The citation included: "For exemplary conduct in ground combat against the armed enemy on or about May 21, 1944." I always felt that I had earned and deserved one but for the other incident and not this one. Oh well!

For the next 10 days it rained almost continuously day and night with about 30 inches total rainfall. It was mud-mud-mud. We were without air or tank support, had great difficulty getting food, water, and ammunition to the front line, and couldn't evacuate the dead and wounded.

As we slogged south there was a large rocky bluff to our left front called the Escarpment. The Japanese there held the high ground and were well entrenched in caves and bunkers. They could see every move we made. It took several days to take and clear this obstacle. The most memorable point of this was that the Japanese 5-inch naval artillery in the caves, that would normally be fired at tanks or other large targets, were lowered down to flat trajectory and fired directly at us. I was carrying a SCR300 radio on my back and had several rounds fired directly at me. If we had had air support or tanks, we could have put them out of business quicker and easier. They were out of range for bazookas and flame throwers and protected from mortar fire, so we had to shoot them down the hard way.

SUGAR LOAF HILL—WESTERN ANCHOR OF THE SHURI DEFENSES (USMC)

After securing and moving on past the Escarpment, we were on or about Bamboo Hill. The weather had lightened up a little, and we were to get our (my) first air support. The Marine air wing flying Corsair fighter planes were to strafe the Japanese front lines before we jumped off. We had our orange luminescent panels laid out to mark our line. Our artillery spotter, Capt. Parker, and I were standing not 3 feet apart when the first

**SUGAR LOAF HILL AND HORSESHOE HILL**
PHOTOGRAPHED AFTER THE BATTLE HAD MOVED ON
INTO MACHISI AND ALMOST TO NAHA. (U.S. ARMY)

plane came in at treetop level. Either the friendly Army-Marine rivalry took a quick turn, or most likely he hit his trigger a hair too soon. He came right through I Company in a hail of 50-caliber machine gun bullets. He hit the artillery captain about waist level, one shot on either side of his spine. His blood and guts showered all over Capt. Parker and me, but neither of us was hit. As far as I know, he was the only one who was hit. As the pilot zoomed on off and swung around to make a second pass, the back-up guys behind us saw what had happened and starting rolling out their orange panels behind us. We quickly got on the radio (which was working) and got the strafing aborted in time. This is what is euphemistically called "friendly fire." The two 50-caliber bullets almost cut him in half. He died a few minutes later, and it sure didn't seem like "friendly fire" to me. I doubt that the pilot ever knew that he had killed our artillery spotter.

The weather stayed clearer. As we were heading southwest toward Keradera, we had a reporter/photographer from the Saturday Evening Post join us. They ran an article, "The 7th Made It The Hard Way," in the magazine. I was standing beside the photographer as he took a picture of our scout, Florencio Quin Bustamonte Preciado, from Superior, Arizona. "Chino," as he was called, got shot in his right hand but later returned to duty.

Later, when I was in the Army Hospital in Modesto, California, I wrote an essay about the next action, which was Horseshoe Hill and the village of Keradera. From the map you can see we were well out ahead of everyone. Our right flank was very vulnerable and exposed, and the left was partially so, but the main Japanese forces were south and west. We took the hill, but that night the Japanese counterattacked and took part of it back. The essay won me a U.S. savings bond and well describes this event. I was told that I Company was awarded a Distinguished Unit Citation for this action. The essay follows:

❖ ❖ ❖ ❖

## UNIT CITATION
### By: Pfc. Holly E. Rees
### I Company, 184th Infantry
### 7th Division, 24th Corps
### 10th Army

Horseshoe Hill! Hill 158! Grid coordinate 67:45! No matter by what name the ground be called, it was just another hurdle that had to be overcome in the race to Tokyo. The time, date, and place are not destined to be remembered. The power and scope of our long years of global warfare will crowd out this story, but to the battle-scarred veterans of this incident on bloody Okinawa, the memory will linger long.

The CO stood just below the crest of Sugar Loaf Hill. With him were the 300 radioman, commo sergeant, and a messenger. Below them lay a peaceful pastoral scene. It had been worked by the Master's hand in the

> 14-May-45
> Okinawa
>
> Dear Mr. Munz,
>
> Imagine me using a typewriter now in a campaign to write letters when I couldn't even find one in the states. The condition of the machine (a portable) and the conditions under which I work are not exactly like a desk job in an office in the states, but it sure beats writing on ~~xxxx~~ a box with a lead pencil.
>
> Several nights ago I happened to run into Gene Hayes. We slept in the same fox-hole that night and had a lot to talk over. The next day we were assigned to our companies. Since he was in a different casual company, we were slightly separated. He is holed in about 200yds. from our company cp where I work. So far he is listed as a rifleman in the 1st squad, 1st platoon of L company. I am a company messenger and clerk in company headquarters of Co. I.
>
> As far as Gene and I know, Bacus is a few hills NW of here but we haven't had time to look him up. His regiment is part of our division and unless he has been wounded etc. he should be here.
> (censored)
> After we left _____ and embarked for parts unknown we were told we would hit Okinawa, Ryukus. We spent the first night ashore in another casual unit and the next day we were assigned to our regiments. We are in the 10th Army, 7th Division, 184th Inf. Regt. so when you read in the news about those units you can be pretty sure about what Hayes, Bacus, and myself are doing.
>
> We were lucky in being assigned to an outfit _____ from the line for a few days rest. This way we get to know most of the fellows in our outfit before we get into combat. A lot of the replacements are rushed right up to an outfit on the line and dont have a chance to know the men in their squad, or talk with the old men and get an understanding of what the thing is going to be like.
>
> Enough about us and nothing about the Okinawa campaign. I want to be sure and get the final edition of the Badger. Since it will be some time before I could write the honorees, I would greatly appreciate it if you would give my congratulations to them. You might tell the graduating seniors that a couple of last years boys out here hope they (PHS 45) have a better deal than our class got after we got out. Tell them to get all they can out of school and their ceremonies and to have a good time while they can—it really means a lot later on.
>
> I guess I had better not tie up the typewriter too long with my personal correspondence so I'll sign off for now.
>
> As ever,
>
> Holly E. Rees    PHS44

LETTER FROM HOLLY REES TO HIS HIGH SCHOOL PRINCIPAL, MAY 1945

gentle greens of fertile hillsides, the browns of bare earth, the greys of the village of Keradera, and the mottled hues of a turbulent sky above. All too soon the red blood and bodies of the men of this command would rend the peaceful picture into the raging hell of a typical battlefield.

The objective of I Company, 184th Infantry—a part of the veteran 7th Division—for May 28, 1945 was to take and hold a small crescent shaped hill about 1500 yards distant. Battalion expected the Japanese resistance to be slight so K and L companies were echeloned to the left rear and a portion of the anti-tank company was assigned to provide rear security.

Argosy and Longacres, artillery units, had given the area a normal barrage and M Company stood ready to throw in some 81mm mortars if any targets of opportunity should arise. Every man carried a full unit of fire for his weapon, which had been cleaned to perfection in readiness for the attack. Yes, it was just another routine drive and then some much-needed rest, stateside even for some veterans with enough points.

The rifle platoons jumped off at 0800. The 2nd pushed down a shallow ravine, crossing a wide, open, valley to the left front. Their objective was to take a long, rounded hill and sweep right and merge with the company above Keradera. The 1st was to sweep around on the right through a small village and attack the right side of the company. Weapons platoon, company CP, and the Reserve 3rd were to push straight ahead and clean out the ground in between.

Shortly after the 2nd moved out, their 536 radio went dead and a costly messenger commo had to be set up. Nip 81s and knee mortars started pasting the frontal area and the 1st reported heavy small-arms and automatic fire. The groups edged ahead by leaps and bounds and by late afternoon the hill was ours.

The bleak, grey sky had darkened and a light rain had started. The men were busy digging-in positions on the perimeter, hoping that the rain would slack up, that they'd get dug-in before it got too dark, and that the supply men could get through with ammo and rations. Just before dark the company jeep pulled in with a load of mortar and 30 caliber ammunition. The mine clearers hadn't caught up and it was too late to make a return for rations and water.

As darkness set in, the men settled down in the rain and mud to await the dawn. Tired and hungry, they peered through the gloom, sensing trouble. Shortly after midnight the Nips counter-attacked, retaking the right half of the hill. This cost us a dozen men, a heavy machine gun, and some ammunition. The rain had let up and the CP was busy trying to contact JASCO to get the lights turned on. The wire to battalion had been knocked out and the 300 radio was wet. At last the artillery radio got through and the Navy 5 inch flares started coming over.

After a bitter fight, the hill was again rendered secure. The next morning was spent in evacuating the dead and wounded, and in getting rations for the tired and hungry men. Later some concertina and trip wire booby traps were put out.

About noon the CO sent the 2nd platoon on a patrol to clear out the hogback that sloped off to the right front. Within an hour they had been driven back with numerous casualties. Machine guns and mortars were thrown in as a base of fire and the 3rd platoon swept around from the right. When the neighboring area had been cleared, a G-3 party made the rounds to determine Nip losses. One hundred and thirty-five Japanese lay scattered over the hillside. "Light resistance" they had called it!

Late that afternoon, forward elements of the 32nd Infantry had pulled up to the right and a 50% guard was ordered for the night. Normal infiltration and a small, but desperate, "Banzai" charge provided some action for the night. Shortly before the 17th Infantry arrived the next day to relieve I Company, the report came through that a full battalion of Japanese Infantry had been dislodged and wiped out in this area. This was one of the last crack outfits to escape destruction when the Naha, Shuri, Yonabaru line broke. Now the Japanese lay in peace (pieces); they were a credit to their emperor, but no match for the fighting men of I Company.

These are the men who fight our wars—fight and die and suffer for the ideals we cherish. They exist in battle as components of fighting units—as teams to score first-down after first-down until the goal-posts in Japan are torn down in victory. These men banded, or were thrust together in common cause and with common goal. Together they have earned a Unit Citation.

❖ ❖ ❖ ❖

After we were relieved at Keradera, we worked our way southeast toward Minatoga on the coast. As I was slogging along in the mud, I saw a piece of wood and almost stepped on it to get one dry step but figured what the heck and went on. The guy behind me about 12-15 feet, named Rich from Panama City, Florida, did step on it, and it was a Japanese land mine. It blew him to smithereens and the force knocked me forward into the mud, but I was not scratched. This was just one of many times that were so close.

When we got to Minatoga, we (our 3rd Battalion) got the assignment to land on Kutaka Island. It was just off the Chinen Peninsula and was blocking the entrance to Nagagasuku Wan and the use of Yonabaru as a port. We loaded on Amtrak vehicles, and after Kutaka had been bombarded by Army and Navy artillery, we landed on Japanese-held

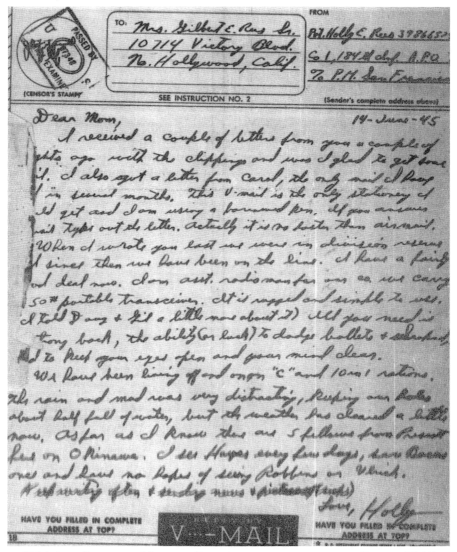

"V-Mail" from Holly Rees to his mother, June 1945

real estate. By nightfall it was cleared. For this we were entitled to wear a bronze arrowhead on our Asiatic Pacific Theater ribbon. In all the books that I have on Okinawa, I haven't ever read any mention of our taking Kutaka, although it is on most of the maps.

After this we moved inland and headed south in the hills west of Gushican. Our main body was on one row of hills, but we had one platoon that had advanced to the next row ahead. It was getting late afternoon and too late for our main force to move ahead. The platoon was cut off and surrounded. The second lieutenant leader and several others were killed and wounded, and their radio was out. Capt. Parker called for volunteers to run the gauntlet to the isolated platoon and help get them back. The radios were unreliable, and I volunteered to run a sound power telephone line to them (with a squad or more of riflemen). We would return in a rolling barrage of 60mm mortar fire. The Japanese were entrenched on the forward side of our hill. We had one of the best mortar men in the business (a hillbilly from South Carolina named Gant), and I felt confidant he'd help get us over and back.

We succeeded in safely getting down the forward side of our hill, across a small valley, and up the hill to the stricken platoon. We gathered up the bodies, wounded and survivors, and made our way back, firing on the Japanese with BAR and moving under the cover of quite close rolling mortar fire. All went well, though we hated to lose the lieutenant as he was well liked by all. He had one of the best Samurai swords I ever saw, and we resolved to get it back to his family. Capt. Parker recommended me for a Bronze Star, and it was rejected since "I was just doing my duty." I was amused when I later got one for Day One and always felt that this was the one I deserved.

We slowly and steadily moved our way southwest over the remaining days. A number of changes had and were occurring. Mainly the weather improved, and the monsoons stopped. The Japanese defenses were more porous. There were still some hills with caves and bunkers but more in between. The tanks and tank flame throwers were now available and effective. The Japanese were worn down and using all personnel on the line but weren't giving up. Finally, on June 21$^{st}$ we found ourselves at the foot of hill 89 in the village of Udo, just southwest of Mabuni. The island was declared secure that day as both the Marines and we had reached the shore on the southern tip of Okinawa.

We had eaten lunch (rations) and were just standing around, feeling secure, when some shots were heard at about 1400. One guy was shot in the leg, the radiator of the company jeep was shot and disabled, and I was shot in the right foot. I always wondered why I was selected (probably because I was the SCR 300 radioman) and appreciated the Japanese policy of shooting to wound us (it would have been easier to shoot me in the head or body, which he could have).

We all dove for our foxholes and were pinned down until we could get a squad around and over the hill to kill their sniper who was in a cave on

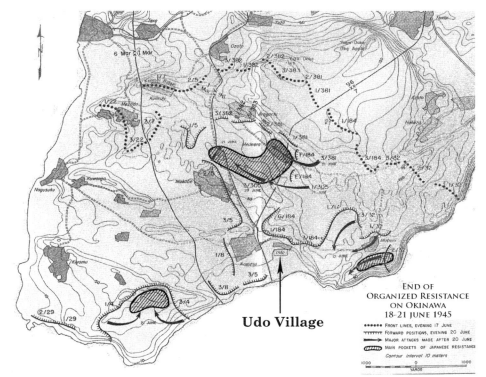

MAP OF FINAL BATTLES. OKINAWA (U.S. ARMY)
HOLLY REES WOUNDED BY JAPANESE SNIPER AT THE FOOT OF HILL 89
NEAR UDO VILLAGE, OKINAWA, JUNE 21ST, 1945

the south side of the hill above us. He had an Arisaka .31-cal. bolt action rifle and was a good shot.

In training we manned the targets on the firing ranges. We stood below the target and pulled it up and down, examined the shot holes, and marked them for the one shooting to see. We quickly developed a sense of sound and could tell which shots were coming at our target or the ones on either side. This is amazing since it was very noisy and there were many targets on the firing line. The point of this digression is that the first thought that popped into my mind when I got hit was "that's my target." I was surprised that a 31-caliber bullet through the instep just in front of the ankle was not more painful than it was. It has caused some problems all my life, but I didn't need any morphine at the time. As I waited to be safely evacuated, I cut and took off my right combat boot, sprinkled sulfa on the wound, and applied a bandage. There was some, but not excessive, bleeding. I know that everyone around me would have gladly traded places with me. I had the "million dollar wound," serious but not fatal or life threatening. This

7th Div Cemetery, Okinawa   145-19

7TH DIV. TEMPORARY CEMETERY, OKINAWA
BODIES LATER RE-INTERRED AT OAHU, HAWAII
(U.S. ARMY SIGNAL CORPS)

was clearly a ticket home and a reprieve from the November landing on the Japanese mainland.

I have to be one of the last battle casualties of WWII. The European theater fighting was over in May 1945 and since I was wounded on June 21, 1945, in the last battle in the Pacific, there were no additional battles fought. Also I am probably one of the youngest surviving combat wounded veterans of WWII, whatever these observations are worth.

Two of the walking wounded on Okinawa head for treatment at an aid station.
(Rickard, J.—8 April 2015, *Walking Wounded on Okinawa*)

# 7

## Wounded, Hospital, and Rehab

*"It was terrifying lying there unable to sleep and fully aware of all that was going on. The atmosphere was tense and the stench horrible. The operating room was a corner of the large area and had curtains, but they were rarely closed."*

**AFTER THEY GOT THE SNIPER AND ALL WAS CLEAR,** Don Kidd and another person (whom I don't remember) got under each of my arms and semi-carried me. I still had my combat boot on my left foot and could hop, so I wasn't just dead weight. I wish I had a video of the procession. Since the company jeep was knocked out, they had to assist me back, probably several hundred yards, until we ran into a makeshift ambulance to carry the other wounded and me back to the battalion aid station (BAS).

At the BAS they determined there was not extensive bleeding, no severe pain or shock, and they ticketed me for transfer back to the regimental aid station. The next vehicle was a larger truck that had racks built on it to hold stretchers and a few seats for the walking wounded. One of the guys, who was naked from the waist down, had a bad wound in his upper inner thigh. He was hyper, waving his genitalia and yelling, "They missed it! They missed it!" He could have been depressed with the serious wound to his thigh and felt that his glass was half empty. Instead, he was ecstatic that his glass was half full.

This reminds me of a friend from Prescott who I ran into later at the Army hospital in Modesto, California. He had been shot in the penis and had been given a prescription spray to use to keep from having an erection so his wound could heal. His favorite joke was about the soldier who had also been shot through the penis and was in a hospital in England. One day the queen was visiting, discussing their wounds and trying to cheer them up. He wouldn't tell the queen where he had been shot. She said she had been married to the king for 30 years and nothing was too personal for her, so he told her he'd been shot in the penis. She said, "Oh! You poor man, I hope it didn't break any bones." He paused a minute and said, "Give my regards to the king."

Another friend from Prescott had never been circumcised, and when he was in the Navy he had the job done. He said he asked the Navy surgeon if he could use pinking shears for the procedure. If I had written this book years ago, I probably would have left out these examples, but today with erectile dysfunction and the treatment thereof touted on prime time TV, it seems more acceptable. These stories are true, except for the queen. But I digress . . .

After further examination and redressing my foot at the regimental aid station, I was sent to a field hospital somewhere in the center of Okinawa. This time my mode of transportation was a Piper Cub airplane. These were used for artillery and intelligence spotting, and some were stripped (like this one) to hold one stretcher for transporting the wounded. I thought all pilots were officers, but mine was a tech sergeant.

By now it was late afternoon or early evening, and this was to be his last flight of the day. We flew basically north over the terrain we had fought over and taken during the past 32 days. The pilot was not in any hurry and obligingly flew back and forth so I could see Keradera, the Escarpment, Yonabaru, etc., on our way to the field hospital.

I arrived at the 68th Field Hospital, somewhere in central Okinawa, about dusk. They carried me in on a stretcher to a large Quonset hut and set me down on the floor. We were more or less lined up in the order in which we arrived but were constantly bumped as more serious cases would be brought in. It was terrifying lying there unable to sleep and fully aware of all that was going on. The atmosphere was tense and the stench horrible. The operating room was a corner of the large area and had curtains, but they were rarely closed.

The doctors' main skill (or one they wanted to develop) was amputations. There were large galvanized garbage cans lined up, and they would saw and cut off arms and legs, throwing them into the garbage cans. Most of the patients had IVs hooked up and received plasma or whole blood, but I didn't.

Finally, early the next morning before first light they got to me. Before even starting to work, they pressured me to sign a consent statement for them to amputate the front half of my right foot. I'd had plenty of time to

TELEGRAM FROM ARMY ADJUTANT GENERAL TO HOLLY'S MOTHER INFORMING HER OF HIS COMBAT INJURY, JULY 1945

observe the MO and calculate the outcome. I knew that without my toes I would be club-footed and would never be able to walk normally. Therefore, I refused to sign the waiver, and the doctor admitted, "They could always take it off later." I know that if I had not been conscious and alert, they would have removed the end of my foot.

After the negotiations and hassle and long wait, they cleaned and dressed the wound and put on a plaster cast. It was not a walking cast and extended up to just below the knee. They left a porthole right above the wound so it could be checked and dressed. Even though a 31-caliber bullet is only about 5/16-inch in diameter, when it traverses through bone and flesh, it creates a much larger path. The wound on my foot was about one-inch wide, one-inch deep and three plus-inches long,

Later I know we were fed and given something to drink, but I have no recollection of details. There were several male doctors, several Army nurses, and some male orderlies, or gophers, busily working the room. I would estimate that several dozen of us were cared for in the 10- to 12-hour period that I was there. As far as I know (and I am confident that I do), I never received any blood or plasma. I did not have excessive bleeding and do not think that I needed any and am confident that I would have if it was needed. In spite of the noise, smell, and confusion, I feel like everyone was professional and competent. By today's medical standards some of our treatment was crude and barbaric, but it was prompt and effective. I am forever grateful that I refused to sign the waiver!

By the time they finished up with me it was about daybreak, and they took me in a regular ambulance (covered and with a red cross on side) to an airfield. I do not know if it was Yontan, Kadena, or another location. We were loaded on a C54 transport plane. The stretchers were locked in along the sides, and there were bucket seats for the walking wounded and other personnel being flown back. The pilot may have had heat, but the cargo area did not. They piled blankets on us on stretchers, but the others were even colder than we were.

Another anxiety was that the ambulatory patients were issued parachutes, but those of us on stretchers were not. I figured that if anything should happen, with the plaster cast on my leg, I'd sink like a rock.

Besides the obvious benefit of being removed from harm's way, there were other reasons to look forward to heading home. I missed family and friends, of course. I couldn't wait to have a clean, warm, dry, safe, and comfortable place to sleep. I especially anticipated eating real eggs and having fresh milk, lettuce, and ice cream—all of which sure beat cold rations.

We landed on Guam, and I was taken to Fleet Hospital 111 where I stayed for a week. Since it was a Navy hospital, most of the patients were Navy or Marines, but there were quite a few Army guys there, too. My cast stayed on the entire time, and they cleaned and dressed the wound through the porthole. As on the troop ships, we usually had Navy beans for breakfast.

Again we were loaded on a C54 for the next leg of our return journey. We made one refueling stop on Johnson Island (it might have been Wake) and landed at Hickam Field on Oahu. They took me by ambulance to the 219th General Hospital at Schofield Barracks near Wahiawa. I stayed there for three weeks, during which time they removed the cast, and a Major Pheasant performed the first surgery on my foot. Toward the end of the time there, they started a whirlpool bath therapy with warm treated water. It bothered me to see the water get pink and red with my blood, but I'm sure I didn't lose much since they never replaced any. There wasn't much to do, or much I could do, and boredom was standard.

**EVACUATION NOTICE TO HOLLY'S MOTHER, JULY 1945**

The final leg of our journey home began as we were taken back to Hickam Field and boarded another C54. On July 23, still on a stretcher, I flew to the Air Debarkation Hospital at Hamilton Field near San Francisco. We stayed there in holding for three days until we could be placed in the regular permanent hospital system. Next I was flown on a C47 to Stockton, California, and then rode by ambulance to Hammond General Hospital at Modesto, California, where I spent the next two months.

During the time there I was more and more ambulatory with crutches and a cane. One time I went swimming, and my scar broke open. (They were all po'd but I was even more so—after all, it was my blood.) As a result, Capt. Morrison performed my second surgery and excised most of the surface scar. They gave me sodium pentothal and said I was getting very amorous with the operating room (OR) nurse.

Much better looking than the OR nurse was an Army nurse, second lieutenant, from Saskatchewan, Canada, whom I dated a few times. I don't think she was supposed to date a private first class, and there wasn't much to do except go to the movies.

One of the wards I was on was a colostomy ward with several dozen colostomy cases and a few other odds and ends. Some were permanent and some were temporary as they repaired some abdominal and rectal problems. The ward stunk! One of the guys and I went to the movie theater, and he constantly elbowed me and asked, "Can you smell anything?" I would gag but try to assure him everything was okay because I felt sorry for him and wanted to see the movie.

One time my mom and dad drove up from North Hollywood to spend the weekend with me. This was the first time they had seen me since before I went overseas. VJ (Victory over Japan) Day happened, and the atom bombs were dropped while I was at Hammond.

The day I arrived at Hammond General Hospital, I ran into Bunky Whelan, who was in our company at Camp Roberts. I also ran into Bob Gardner, from Prescott, who was a patient there too. My buddy Gene Hayes was sent to William Beaumont General Hospital in El Paso, Texas, and he received a medical discharge because of his leg wound. Due to either nerve or muscle damage, he had "drop foot" and had to wear a special shoe and leg brace on that leg.

My foot had healed about all it was going to. Since my rehabilitation was complete, I was determined to be fit for "limited duty" and sent packing.

## CORRESPONDENCE

The only people that I corresponded with were my parents and my girlfriend. Between them I probably got one or two letters a week and I didn't get home with any of their letters.

While the 7th Infantry Division was in division reserve, I borrowed the company portable typewriter and wrote a letter to my high school principal. He saved it and gave it to me after I got home.

Later, in combat, we had "mail call" and received mail most evenings. We wrote when we could, which was unpredictable. The preferred way of writing was "V mail," which was photographed and the film flown back to the states and printed out and mailed. Mom saved one of the V mail notes I sent that was written on June 14, 1945, a week before I was shot.

The correspondence that no one wanted to get was "The Telegram." Luckily, I had already phoned my parents from the Oahu Hospital, and told them I had been wounded. It was nearly a month after I was shot that they received "The Telegram," the official War Department notice that I had been wounded.

The final correspondence was a postcard sent from the 219th General Hospital on Oahu telling my parents that I was "evacuated to the United States on July 22."

Soldiers and Marines stormed the beaches with the help of amphibian crafts as heavy support fire from Navy battleships blanketed the beaches with smoke and dust at the beginning of the Battle of Okinawa.
(U.S. Army)

# 8

## 7TH INFANTRY ON OKINAWA: COMBAT OBSERVATIONS

*"You can get a little of the flavor of combat by watching Band of Brothers, Saving Private Ryan and other good war films. Many others glorify and distort the picture. None of them, however, can do justice to the unmitigated hell that is infantry combat."*

**THE BREAKDOWN OF THE 7TH INFANTRY DIVISION'S** time on Okinawa was: 40 days from landing to relief, 10 days in division reserve and 32 days combat until the island was declared secure. I was with them for the reserve time and final 32 days.

The troop strength of the 7th ID varied from way below 15,000 up to 17,263 plus attached and support elements. Casualities for the 7th were as follows:

**Killed:** 636    First 40 days    **Wounded:** 2,817    First 40 days
         486    Last 32 days                  2,126    Last 32 days
     1,122    Total                            4,943    Total

\* **Non-battle:** 2,212    First 40 days
                    2,613    Last 32 days
                    4,825    Total

*\*(Non-battle: Includes accidental physical injury as well as what is now known as "post traumatic stress disorder". In WWI this phenomenon was called "shell shock"—we called it "battle fatigue." They are basically all the same. Even though our time in combat time was actually less during the second phase of the campaign, the psychological effects were cumulative, so the PTSD casualties were higher.)*

**Total Casualties:** 5,681    First 40 days
                            5,212    Last 32 days
                         10,893    Total

I was reminded of the rather prophetic things we were told in basic training that proved quite accurate. We had about 10% killed, 25% wounded and many others injured (non combat) and stricken by battle fatigue.

During the 82 days of combat 110,000 Japanese were killed for a daily average of 1,341. The "kill ratio" of 12,520 Americans killed to the 110,000 enemy meant that 8.786 of the enemy were KIA for every American KIA.

The 10th Army Artillery expended 2,116,691 rounds of all sizes. This averaged 25,813 rounds per day of combat and 19,242 rounds per enemy killed.

The following 4 expenditures are for just the 24th Army Corps and do not include the III Amphib. Corps. They are compared to days of combat and enemy killed, and even though they are less than the 10th Army figures, they help to illustrate the magnitude of armament used:

| | | |
|---|---|---|
| **Mortar:** | 964,890 | 11,767 per day |
| | | *8.77 per enemy killed* |
| **Rifle:** | 9,267,923 | 113,023 per day |
| | | *84.25 per enemy killed* |
| **Machine Gun:** | 17,072,253 | 208,198 per day |
| (.30 & .50 cal.) | | *155.2 per enemy killed* |
| **Hand Grenade:** | 366,734 | 4,472 per day |
| | | *3.34 per enemy killed* |

There was, and is, a deep-seated loyalty and sense of belonging in each branch and unit of the military service. This usually manifests itself in the conviction (often expressed) that "my outfit was the best in the Army," etc. Interestingly, it is not so much an ego thing that "I'm the best" but a respect for fellow soldiers and a collective loyalty. This is true at all levels with an increasing intensity as you get to smaller and smaller units. Thus Army loyalty is high, infantry loyalty higher, 7th Division still higher, 184th Infantry Regiment still higher, I Company the highest. The "Band of Brothers" bonding and affection syndrome is very evident at the small unit level.

The friendly rivalry between Army and Marines is often exaggerated and misunderstood. Both consist of combat troops and a lot of "rear echelon" personnel. Most all combat veterans, regardless of branch or unit, have a deep respect, loyalty and affection for each other. It is mainly the non-combat people who create the conflicts and arguments.

The loyalty, support thing applies to personnel as well as units. I know that Capt. James Parker, from Eureka, California, was the best infantry company commander, that Gant was the best 60mm mortar man, that Glick and Waldowski were the best medics, etc. Of course, there were a few SOB's that you couldn't stand or who were incompetent (both officers and enlisted men), but we learned to live with that, too.

One thing that helped level the playing field, but certainly not for that reason, was that in combat no one near the front line wore insignia and saluting was absolutely forbidden. It was a little difficult to go into the Army and get steeped in the caste, officer-enlisted men, system. Then we would go into combat and ignore, repress it; then turn it back on when out of combat. More so to the Japs than us, the officers were prime targets, along with radiomen, artillery spotters, machine gunners, mortar men, etc. Of course, the officers had to be extremely careful with binoculars, maps and anything else that would reveal their status. The Japs feared and were more impressed by their officers than we were. We often felt that we were as good as, or better than, some of our officers. But of course, we "saluted the uniform and not the man."

You can get a little of the flavor of combat by watching *Band of Brothers*, *Saving Private Ryan* and other good war films. Many other films glorify and distort the picture. None of them, however, can do justice to the unmitigated hell that is infantry combat. It is one thing to sit in a theater or your living room and watch what is fairly well presented, and another to be in the middle of the action with your life constantly in mortal danger. The rain, snow, extreme heat or cold, volume of noise, smell (blood, death, gun smoke) as well as the usual state of sleep deprivation, exhaustion and fear make the actual experience almost beyond imagination or words to describe it. The movies tend to show brief encounters fairly well, but in actual combat the action is often continuous and goes on day and night.

There is almost always "a lot of metal in the air," and the adage that "what goes up must come down" is clearly at play. The anti-aircraft fire, from the enemy, offshore naval units or ours back from the front, all produce a lot of flak that has to fall somewhere—often on the front.

Artillery fire, mortars, hand grenades and small arms fire are deadliest at close range but produce peripheral shrapnel in a larger general area. It really doesn't matter whether any of this is "friendly" or enemy fire, the nuisance and/or danger is the same. To get a small grasp of the scope of all this (which is without saying, many times worse for the Japs), we fired 1,766,352 rounds of all sizes of artillery, mostly 105mm, the Navy fired 600,018 rounds of all types of shells in land support (not including the ones fired at Jap ships and planes), the 24th Army Corps alone fired 9,267,923 rounds of 30-caliber rifle ammunition and 16,285,499 rounds of 30-caliber machine gun ammo. The usage varied, but just the average of these for the 82 days of combat were: 113,023 rounds of rifle shells per day and 198,604 rounds of machine gun ammo per day.

Sleep, if any, was usually deficient. You learned to sleep when you could in a fox-hole sitting. The Japs counter-attacked at night or simply infiltrated our lines. The worst were Banzai attacks during the night. At the worst no one got any sleep, and at the best we took turns while some slept and some stood guard. When the stuff hit the fan we were all involved.

Hygiene! We would go for days with out shaving or brushing our teeth. One time they set up showers well back from the front. The old timers declined but being green and naïve, I walked back for a shower. There were no clean clothes, and by the time I got back to the company, you couldn't tell I had showered. We tried to change underwear and socks (back and forth with the same 2 pairs) and "dry wash" them before putting them back on. This was marginal at best, and even this was not always possible. I wore the same fatigue pants and coat and combat boots for the entire 32 days of combat. Naturally, with this lack of hygiene and the vast amounts of rain and mud and wet feet, there were many foot problems. We had some government issue foot powder that may have helped some.

Bathroom (i.e., toilet) facilities were non-existent, and you couldn't always "go" when you needed to. It was always Army protocol to dig a hole and cover your mess.

Dead bodies, mostly Japs, were a constant irritation, if they were even a day or so old, they were bloated, stinking and crawling with maggots. We tried to avoid them, but sometimes when you were pinned down and in close proximity you couldn't do much.

Although it made no immediate change for us, we celebrated the news of victory in Europe. The main hope was that troops would be transferred from Europe to the Pacific, and we would have some help with the landings on Japan scheduled for November 1945.

A FEW YARDS BEHIND THE FRONT LINES ON OKINAWA, FIGHTING MEN OF THE US ARMYS 77TH INFANTRY DIVISION LISTEN TO RADIO REPORTS OF GERMANY'S SURRENDER ON MAY 8, 1945. THEIR BATTLE-HARDENED FACES INDICATE THE IMPASSIVENESS WITH WHICH THEY RECEIVED THE NEWS OF THE VICTORY ON A FAR DISTANT FRONT. ONE MINUTE AFTER THIS PHOTO WAS TAKEN, THEY RETURNED TO THEIR COMBAT POST, OFFICIALLY HOWEVER, AMERICAN FORCES ON OKINAWA CELEBRATED THE END OF THE WAR IN EUROPE BY TRAINING EVERY SHIP AND SHORE BATTERY ON A JAPANESE TARGET AND FIRING ONE SHELL SIMULTANEOUSLY AND PRECISELY AT MIDNIGHT. (NATIONAL ARCHIVES, FA 41224- FA)

Most soldiers acquired souvenirs, but we had to be selective because of space and weight. Many were for our own personal keepsakes, but some got items to sell to the rear echelon Army or the Navy and air corps guys. We had to carefully guard the ones we wanted to keep them from being stolen.

I got home with a nice Arisaka 31-caliber rifle and bayonet. Later just before I got married, I sold the rifle to my brother. He had it re-chambered to fit American cartidges. I still have the bayonet. I also have a particular type of "Rising Sun" Japanese flag that I took off one of the first enemy soldiers I shot. I will talk more about the flag in a later chapter. I cut the one star insignia off the collar of another enemy and still have it.

At night I would use a belt and tie the rifle to my thigh (while in the hospital and transportation) and often woke up as someone was trying to steal it. Also, some officers tried to confiscate the rifle "for military intelligence or training" but obviously for themselves, but they didn't succeed.

I regret not keeping the rifle and always was sorry that I didn't get a nice officer's sword and some Japanese binoculars.

# 9

## Post-Hospital Military

*"All this, plus some medals and decorations, and I was still seven months shy of my 21st birthday. I could serve, fight, and get wounded, but I still couldn't vote or legally buy alcohol."*

**I WAS RELEASED FROM HAMMOND GENERAL** Hospital on September 25th and sent to Fort Mac Arthur, California, for three days. Then I was given about six weeks of TDR&R, temporary duty for rest and relaxation. This ran from September 28th until November 15th. I first went to see my parents in North Hollywood, California, and three things come to mind about this time.

The first memory is Gil's wife, Dorothy, was mucho pregnant and living with my folks while Gil was on his way home from a second tour of duty in the Pacific. While I was there, she went into labor, so early one evening we took her to a hospital in Glendale, California. While Mom was with Dorothy in the labor area, Dad and I waited in a reception area. There were lots of young military guys waiting for their wives to deliver. While the others were smoking, drinking, pacing the floor, and visiting, I sat calmly reading a magazine. Some of the guys couldn't stand it and finally approached me to ask how I could possibly be so calm and indifferent during such an eventful time. Later that evening on October 11th, my niece Yvonne Rees was born.

A second memory is of a neighbor of my parents having large wooden barrels in a garage and they were making dill pickles. They stunk, foamed, and spoiled me on dill pickles for years.

The third memory is of one day sitting at the kitchen table eating a late breakfast, Mom and Dad were both at work, and I was there alone. There was a single light hanging above the table about 6 inches from the wall. Suddenly I heard a low rumble and felt a mild vibration and then noticed the gap between the table and wall was varying in width. Also, the hanging light above was swinging in an arc. I had just experienced my first, and only, earthquake.

I went on to Prescott, Arizona, where I visited a few days. I borrowed a car and drove over to Jerome to watch a basketball game. Then I drove on to Glendale to visit my Uncle Si and other relatives. He loaned me his car and I drove to Tucson, visited the University of Arizona, and watched a football game. After returning to Phoenix I boarded a train for San Antonio, Texas. When the train got to El Paso, it stopped and all the Negroes had to go to the back of the train. This was my first glimpse of Jim Crow and the segregated South.

I made it on schedule and reported in at the Army Ground and Service Forces Redistribution Center (AGSFRC) at Fort Sam Houston, Texas, on November 15th. When soldiers returned from overseas or were discharged from the hospitals, they were screened. If they had enough points they went to a separation center for discharge. Points were credited for length of service, time overseas, time in combat, and medals received. Those without enough points were sent to the AGSFRC for reassignment. Since the war was over in both Europe and the Pacific by now, most were placed in the continental United States, but some could be sent back for occupation duties. I was a transient at the center for 13 days. During this time we had interviews, evaluations, lectures, and a relaxed time of waiting. On November 28th I was selected to stay on at the center and was assigned to the Information and Education Branch. Fort Sam was the only place I was ever stationed that had permanent, masonry buildings. Our barracks were multi-story, and we had a PX in the basement. The only problem was the juke box blaring, especially in the evenings. The song played the most was San Antonio Rose and I got tired of it. I was promoted from private first class to corporal and stayed at the center from November 28th until February 28th, when it was closed.

Our main function in the Information and Education Branch was to handle United States Armed Forces Institute (USAFI) courses. The war department had contracted with the University of Wisconsin (UW) in Madison to administer the USAFI. They reprinted most of the UW textbooks into paperback and had a large number of correspondence courses available. Everything was free, the courses flexible, and could, upon completion, lead to college credits. When we finally shut down, I obtained a number of these textbooks, which I still have.

The sergeant in charge of the Information and Education section was from Wisconsin, and he had arranged for a visit to the USAFI headquarters in Madison. Just before it was to happen, they lowered the points needed for discharge. He became eligible and was out of there. No one else was interested in the trip so I volunteered. From December 14th until December 25th I was on detached service to attend the meetings in Madison. I got hold of an overcoat and rode the train from San Antonio to St. Louis to Chicago, changed stations, and took another train to Madison.

Going from San Antonio to Madison in December was culture shock and weather shock big time. The temperature barely got up to zero in the daytime and was way below zero at night. There were about 25 of us there from all over the United States, and I was the only enlisted man (a corporal). The officers were snotty and thought I was there to be their lackey. Luckily a captain from Fort Bliss in El Paso took me under his wing, told them off, and cleared the air. Madison and the University of Wisconsin were beautiful, and I not only got a lot out of the meetings but thoroughly enjoyed the time there. On the way back, I stopped in St. Louis and went to a suburb, Webster Groves, to visit a friend, Bob Theiss, whom I had met at the 219th General Hospital on Oahu.

Another activity at the Information and Education Branch was every Thursday night we had a big orientation meeting open to anyone (i.e., not mandatory). We had a keg of beer and a bountiful supply of breads, cheese, and cold cuts. We did have some discussions to partly justify these gatherings. I quickly learned that the best part was to check out a jeep, go to the Pearl Brewery that afternoon, and the next morning to pick up and return the keg. They had a tap room with plenty of free beer. The delicatessen was not nearly as interesting but essential. The three months with the Information and Education Branch were an interesting and enjoyable time, and several memories include the following:

One of the guys was Peterson, with whom I had trained at Camp Roberts. His father was a Red Cross representative at Camp Swift near Bastrop. One weekend I went with him to visit his parents and occasionally he would borrow his dad's car. Another buddy was Bill Keith, who had been with "The Big Red One"—the 1st Infantry Division. We hit it off well and hung out a lot.

Another guy (who will remain anonymous) was dating a very attractive Hispanic girl, and their sex life was legendary. One night she called the barracks for someone to come and get him, stating that he had passed out on her after a marathon session. It should come as no surprise that he was affectionately known as "The Rabbit."

Another guy married a local girl and began looking awful. It seems that she thought her parents had had sex only four times because there were four children. Since he was still in the Army, they didn't want to start a family so that meant no sex. After several weeks he went to her mother with his problem. She thought it was hilarious and said she'd talk to her daughter. She explained to the daughter that she and her father had a very long and active sex life. Yes, sex was for procreation but was good for a lot more! The guy's wife went along with her mother's suggestion and *loved* it. He drove the unit's jeep, and she would call him during the day with some excuse for him to come home. He again started looking haggard.

Some time later she had an appendectomy. They goofed and left some gauze packing in that should have been removed. It became infected and she almost died. Along with a few others in the outfit, I went downtown to Santa Rosa Hospital and donated blood for her. This was the first of many times that I gave blood.

The climate in San Antonio was mild, and one of our favorite activities was to borrow or rent bicycles and explore Fort Sam Houston or ride to nearby Breckenridge Park. We enjoyed the exercise and seeing the zoo, oriental gardens, and other sights.

HOLLY AND POST-WAR SERVICE COLLEAGUES, RIDING BYCYCLES IN BRECKENRIDGE PARK, SAN ANTONIO, TEXAS 1945 04 '46

As the flow of returnees dwindled and our work diminished, we eventually closed the AGSFR center. For a month, February 28 to March 28th, I was assigned to the supply room. Then, from March 28th until June 27th (another three month long assignment), I was assigned to the main file and records section at post headquarters. Here I was promoted to sergeant and learned the Dewey Decimal System. The work was interesting and detailed. When there were lulls, it was fun to read some of the files. This was the first time I had been exposed to the regular Army syndrome—all the others were citizen soldiers and planned to get out and not make an Army career.

The point system was still in effect, but it was steadily becoming a matter of just time in service. During the late spring the magic number for discharge was 24 months. Since my 24 months wouldn't be up until September 23rd, and since I wanted to start college at the University of Arizona in the fall, I was very anxious. Luckily, in late June they lowered the number to 21 months (which I had on June 23rd) and my Army career was on the skids.

On June 27th I transferred to the Separation Center at Fort Sam Houston, and on June 29th I received my discharge from the Army of the United States. My total service time was 21 months and seven days. I had spent exactly four months overseas, or outside the continental U.S., 32 days in combat, and three months in the hospital.

All this, plus some medals and decorations, and I was still seven months shy of my 21st birthday. I could serve, fight and get wounded, but I still couldn't vote or legally buy alcohol.

### SUMMARY—Itinerary—Assignments

| From | To | What | Where |
| --- | --- | --- | --- |
| | 09-23-44 | Induction Station | Phoenix, AZ |
| 09-24-44 | 10-03-44 | Reception Center | Fort Mac Arthur, CA |
| 10-03-44 | 02-09-45 | IRTC | Camp Roberts, CA |
| 02-09-45 | 02-21-45 | Delay-in-route | No. Hollywood—Prescott |
| 02-21-45 | 03-07-45 | Overseas Rept. Depot | Fort ORD, CA |
| 03-07-45 | 03-09-45 | Troop Train | |
| 03-09-45 | 03-22-45 | Port of Embarkation | Fort Lewis, WA |

| From | To | What | Where |
|---|---|---|---|
| 03-22-45 | 03-31-45 | Troop Ship | *SS Aquaprince* |
| 03-31-45 | 04-07-45 | AGF Rept. Depot #13 | Oahu, HI |
| 04-07-45 | 04-27-45 | Troop Ship | *USS Bottineau* |
| 04-27-45 | 05-01-45 | AGF Rept. Depot #23 | Saipan, Marianas Islands |
| 05-01-45 | 05-09-45 | Assault Troop Ship | A.P.A. 235 |
| 05-10-45 | 06-21-45 | Co.I, 184th Infantry | Okinawa, Ryukyu Islands |

(Received.. gun shot wound in right foot at 1400, 21 June 1945 and evacuated wounded in action)

| From | To | What | Where |
|---|---|---|---|
| 06-21-45 | 06-22-45 | 68th Field Hospital | Okinawa |
| 06-22-45 | 06-23-45 | NATS hospital plane | (C-54) |
| 06-22-45 | 06-29-45 | Fleet Hospital III | Guam, Marianas Islands |
| 06-29-45 | 06-29-45 | ATC hospital plane | (C-54) |
| 06-29-45 | 07-22-45 | 219th General Hospital | Oahu, HI |
| 07-22-45 | 07-23-45 | Air Evacuation ward | Hickam Field, Oahu, HI |

| From | To | What | Where |
|---|---|---|---|
| 07-23-45 | 07-23-45 | ATC hospital plane | (C-54) |
| 07-23-45 | 07-26-45 | Air Debarkation Hospital | Hamilton Field, CA |
| 07-26-45 | 07-26-45 | ATC cargo plane | (C-47) |
| 07-26-45 | 09-25-45 | Hammond General Hospital | Modesto, CA |
| 09-25-45 | 09-28-45 | WD Personnel Center | Fort MacArthur, CA |
| 09-28-45 | 11-15-45 | TDR&R | California & Arizona |
| 11-15-45 | 11-28-45 | AG & SF Red. Station | Fort Sam Houston, TX |
| 09-28-45 | 02-28-46 | I&E Branch Station | Fort Sam Houston, TX |
| 12-14-45 | 12-25-46 | Detached Service USAF I | Madison, WI |

| | | | |
|---|---|---|---|
| 02-02-46 | 03-28-46 | Supply Room, AGSFR5 | Fort Sam Houston, TX |
| 03-28-46 | 06-27-46 | Main File &Records Sec. Post Headquarters | Fort Sam Houston, TX |
| 06-27-46 | 06-29-46 | Separation Center | Fort Sam Houston, TX |

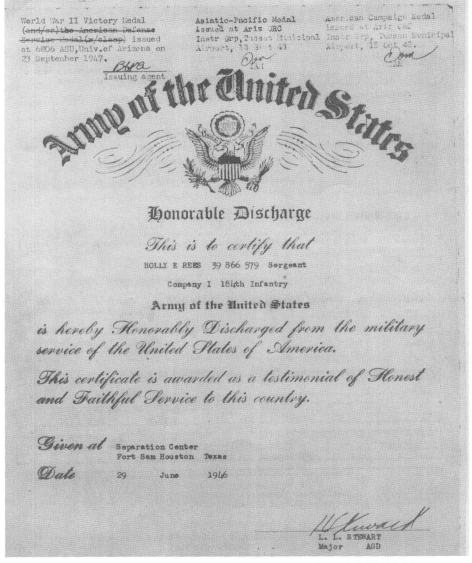

HOLLY E. REES HONORABLE DISCHARGE, JUNE 1946 (front)

## ENLISTED RECORD AND REPORT OF SEPARATION
## HONORABLE DISCHARGE

| 1. LAST NAME - FIRST NAME - MIDDLE INITIAL | 2. ARMY SERIAL NO. | 3. GRADE | 4. ARM OR SERVICE | 5. COMPONENT |
|---|---|---|---|---|
| REES HOLLY E | 39 866 579 | SGT 31May46 | INF | AUS |

| 6. ORGANIZATION | 7. DATE OF SEPARATION | 8. PLACE OF SEPARATION |
|---|---|---|
| Company I 184th Infantry | 29 June 46 | Separation Center Fort Sam Houston Texas |

| 9. PERMANENT ADDRESS FOR MAILING PURPOSES | 10. DATE OF BIRTH | 11. PLACE OF BIRTH |
|---|---|---|
| 10714 Victory Blvd North Hollywood Los Angeles Co Calif | 21 Jan 26 | Prescott Ariz |

| 12. ADDRESS FROM WHICH EMPLOYMENT WILL BE SOUGHT | 13. COLOR EYES | 14. COLOR HAIR | 15. HEIGHT | 16. WEIGHT | 17. NO. DEPEND. |
|---|---|---|---|---|---|
| See 9 | Blue | Blonde | 6' 0" | 175 LBS. | 0 |

| 18. RACE | 19. MARITAL STATUS | 20. U.S. CITIZEN | 21. CIVILIAN OCCUPATION AND NO. |
|---|---|---|---|
| WHITE X | SINGLE X | YES X | Student High School Academic X-0 |

### MILITARY HISTORY

| 22. DATE OF INDUCTION | 23. DATE OF ENLISTMENT | 24. DATE OF ENTRY INTO ACTIVE SERVICE | 25. PLACE OF ENTRY INTO SERVICE |
|---|---|---|---|
| 23 Sept 44 | - | 23 Sept 44 | Ind Sta Phoenix Ariz |

| SELECTIVE SERVICE DATA | 26. REGISTERED | 27. LOCAL S.S. BOARD NO. | 28. COUNTY AND STATE | 29. HOME ADDRESS AT TIME OF ENTRY INTO SERVICE |
|---|---|---|---|---|
| X | YES | 1 | Yavapai Co Ariz | 138 N Virginia St Prescott Yavapai Co Ariz |

| 30. MILITARY OCCUPATIONAL SPECIALTY AND NO. | 31. MILITARY QUALIFICATION AND DATE |
|---|---|
| Clerk Typist 405 | Combat Infantryman Badge (21 May 45) |

**32. BATTLES AND CAMPAIGNS**
Ryukyus GO 105 WD 45

**33. DECORATIONS AND CITATIONS**
American Theater Campaign Ribbon Asiatic Pacific Theater Campaign Ribbon With 1 Bronze Star Good Conduct Medal Purple Heart Medal GO 286 Hq Control Pacific Base Com'd 5 July 45 Victory Ribbon Central

**34. WOUNDS RECEIVED IN ACTION**
AP 21 June 45

| 35. LATEST IMMUNIZATION DATES | | | | 36. SERVICE OUTSIDE CONTINENTAL U. S. AND RETURN | | |
|---|---|---|---|---|---|---|
| SMALLPOX | TYPHOID | TETANUS | OTHER (specify) | DATE OF DEPARTURE | DESTINATION | DATE OF ARRIVAL |
| 19Nov45 | 19Nov45 | 1Nov44 | 13March45 Typhus | 22 March 45 | AP | 31 March 45 |

| 37. TOTAL LENGTH OF SERVICE | | | | | 38. HIGHEST GRADE HELD | | | |
|---|---|---|---|---|---|---|---|---|
| CONTINENTAL SERVICE | | | FOREIGN SERVICE | | | | | |
| YEARS | MONTHS | DAYS | YEARS | MONTHS | DAYS | | | |
| 1 | 5 | 5 | 0 | 4 | 2 | SGT | 22 July 45 | US | 23 July 45 |

**39. PRIOR SERVICE**
None

**40. REASON AND AUTHORITY FOR SEPARATION**
Convenience of the Government (RR 1-1 Demobilization) AR 615-365 15 Dec 44

| 41. SERVICE SCHOOLS ATTENDED | 42. EDUCATION (Years) | | |
|---|---|---|---|
| None | Grammar 8 | High School 4 | College 0 |

### PAY DATA You 6908

| 43. LONGEVITY FOR PAY PURPOSES | 44. MUSTERING OUT PAY | 45. SOLDIER DEPOSITS | 46. TRAVEL PAY | 47. TOTAL AMOUNT | NAME OF DISBURSING OFFICER |
|---|---|---|---|---|---|
| YEARS 1 | MONTHS | DAYS 7 | TOTAL $300 | THIS PAYMENT $100 | None | $39.70 | $213.27 | B. JEFFREY Lt Col FD |

### INSURANCE NOTICE
IMPORTANT IF PREMIUM IS NOT PAID WHEN DUE OR WITHIN THIRTY-ONE DAYS THEREAFTER, INSURANCE WILL LAPSE. MAKE CHECKS OR MONEY ORDERS PAYABLE TO THE TREASURER OF THE U. S. AND FORWARD TO COLLECTIONS SUBDIVISION, VETERANS ADMINISTRATION, WASHINGTON 25, D. C.

| 48. KIND OF INSURANCE | 49. HOW PAID | 50. Effective Date of Allotment Discontinuance | 51. Date of Next Premium Due (One month after 50) | 52. PREMIUM DUE EACH MONTH | 53. INTENTION OF VETERAN TO |
|---|---|---|---|---|---|
| Nat. Serv. X | U.S. Govt. | None | Allotment X | Direct to V. A. | 30 June 46 | 31 July 46 | $6.50 | Continue | Continue Only | Discontinue X |

**55. REMARKS** (This space for completion of above items or entry of other items specified in W. D. Directives)

FOR CONVENIENCE, A CERTIFICATE OF ELIGIBILITY NO 2639888 HAS BEEN ISSUED BY THE VETERANS ADMINISTRATION TO BE USED FOR THE FUTURE REQUEST OF Lapel Button Issued 15 June 46 INSURANCE BENEFIT UNDER TITLE III OF THE SERVICEMEN'S READ-ASR Score (2 Sept 45) JUSTMENT ACT OF 1944, AS AMENDED, THAT MAY BE AVAILABLE TO THE PERSON TO WHOM THIS SEPARATION PAPER WAS ISSUED.

| 56. SIGNATURE OF PERSON BEING SEPARATED | 57. PERSONNEL OFFICER (Type name, grade and organization - signature) |
|---|---|
| Holly E Rees | M. L. CLIFTON CWO USA Ass't Mil Pers Officer |

HOLLY E. REES HONORABLE DISCHARGE, JUNE 1946 (back)

Certificate from the National D-Day Museum in New Orleans, Lousiana for a brick set in their "Road to Victory" walk commemorating Holly E. Rees's service in combat on Okinawa with his division.

U.S.S. PRINCETON, 1944

# 10

## U.S. Navy Aircraft Carriers & Aircraft

*"During its active life of 17 months, the USS Princeton traveled about 150,000 miles or about 300 miles a day average. Crews from the USS Princeton shot down 186 Japanese planes in aerial combat and seven more by anti-aircraft fire. They sank or crippled 17 ships as well as damaged land targets."*

**DURING WORLD WAR II THE UNITED STATES NAVY** had 129 aircraft carriers on line (available for use). These were of three main types: the regular (large) CVs, the "light" or medium CVLs, and the small escort carriers or CVEs.

At the time the Japanese attacked Pearl Harbor we had only seven aircraft carriers:

| | | | |
|---|---|---|---|
| CV 1 | *USS Langley* | (class) | commissioned March 1920 |
| 2 | *USS Lexington* | (class) | commissioned December 1927 |
| 3 | *USS Saratoga* | (Lex cl) | commissioned November 1927 |
| 4 | *USS Ranger* | (class) | commissioned June 1934 |
| 5 | *USS Yorktown* | (class) | commissioned September 1937 |
| 6 | *USS Enterprise* | (YT cl) | commissioned May 1938 |
| 7 | *USS Wasp* | (class) | commissioned April 1940 |
| 8 | *USS Hornet* | (YT cl) | commissioned October 1941 |

As hostilities began, it was obvious that many more aircraft carriers would be needed to pursue and win the war. The CVs were large, expensive, and slow to build. The CV9 USS Essex (class) was the first commissioned in 1942 followed by CVs 10 to 47 through May 1946. These Essex class carriers (CV order) were: *Yorktown, Intrepid, Hornet, Franklin, Ticonderoga, Randolph, Lexington, Bunker Hill, Wasp, Hancock, Bennington, Boxer, Bon Homme Richard, Leyte, Kearsarge, Antietam, Princeton, Shangra-la, Lake Champlain, Tarawa, Valley Forge* and *Philippine Sea*. CV 34, the *USS Oriskany* was commissioned September 1950.

Large carriers, which would have been valuable in the attack on Japan, came on line after the actual hostilities of WWII were over. These three were:

    CV 41 *USS Midway* (class)      commissioned September 1945
    42 *USS Franklin D. Roosevelt*      commissioned October 1945
    43 *USS Coral Sea*      commissioned October 1947

Because the CVs would be slow to produce and bring on line, a plan developed to add a carrier flight deck on a cruiser hull and produce a smaller "light" carrier. Built on a Cleveland class cruiser hull, the first CVL was the *USS Independence* (class) CVL 22. The following eight CVLs, all commissioned in 1943, were:

    CVL 23 *USS Princeton*
    24 *USS Belleau Wood*
    25 *USS Cowpens*
    26 *USS Monterrey*
    27 *USS Langley*
    28 *USS Cabot*
    29 *USS Bataan*
    30 *USS San Jacinto*

Of particular interest to me were the following three CVLs.

1. The *USS Princeton* CVL 23. My brother Gilbert served on the *USS Princeton* from May 1944 until it was sunk on October 24, 1944, in Air Group 27.

2. The *USS Independence* CVL 22. Air Group 27 was reassembled and served on the *Independence* from June 1945 until the hostilities were over and Japan surrendered.

3. The *USS San Jacinto* CVL 30. President George H. W. Bush flew an Avenger TBM off the *San Jacinto* until he was shot down and ditched at sea (to be picked up by a submarine). At his presidential library and museum, here in Bryan/College Station, Texas they have a scale model of the *San Jacinto* and a real, restored Avenger.

Independence Class CVL statistics:
Nine of these light aircraft carriers were built between January 1943 and December 1943. Alphabetically: *Bataan, Belleau Wood, Cabot, Cowpens, Independence, Langley, Monterrey, Princeton* and *San Jacinto*.

Built by New York Shipbuilding (Camden, New Jersey) on Cleveland class light cruiser hulls

Displacement: 10,650 tons standard/14,900 tons deep load
Length: 600 ft. long at water line/622'6" overall
Beam: 71'6"
Draught: 21' standard/24'6" deep load
Aircraft: 30; 12 fighter, 9 dive bombers, 9 torpedo bombers
Flight deck: 552 ft x 73 ft
Armament: 24 40mm and 16 20mm guns
Machinery: 4 boilers, GE geared steam turbines, 4 shafts
Stacks: 4 outboard on right (starboard) side
Power: 74,600 KW/100,000 shp
Speed: 31.5 knots
Fuel: 2,600 tons
Range: 12,500 km @ 15 knots
Armour: 83-127mm and 50mm protective deck
Complement: 1,500 men

The *USS Princeton* was named for the battle of *Princeton* on January 3, 1777. Earlier aircraft carriers were named after battles, but later ones were named after people; examples include *Franklin D. Roosevelt, Forrestal, Abraham Lincoln,* and *Nimitz*.

The *USS Princeton* was christened by Mrs. Harold Dodds, wife of the president of Princeton University with the customary champagne.

During its active life of 17 months, the *USS Princeton* traveled about 150,000 miles or about 300 miles a day average. Crews from the *USS Princeton* shot down 186 Japanese planes in aerial combat and seven more by anti-aircraft fire. They sank or crippled 17 ships as well as other damaged land targets.

While Gil was with Air Group 27 on the *USS Princeton*, he earned three battle stars. I am not sure how many AG 23 earned.

Earliest tactics were largely hit and run, but later with enlarged fleet participation and support vessels the attacks were more sustained.

The first commander of the *USS Princeton* was Capt. George R. Henderson (February 25, 1943 to February 8, 1944) with Air Group 23 aboard. The second commander was Capt. William H. Buracker (February 8, 1944 to October 24, 1944) with AG 27 aboard. Capt. John M. Hoskins was scheduled to be the third captain and lost a leg when the *USS Princeton* was bombed and sunk.

The commander of Air Group 23 was Cdr. H. L. Miller, and Lt. Cdr. E. W. Wood, Jr. led AG 27 until he was killed on a mission. Later Lt. J. G. Dooling was the leader of AG 27, and H. L. Stalnaker was the executive officer.

Many of the early air groups bore the same number as their carriers. For instance, AG 16 was on the CV 16, the *USS Lexington*, and AG 23 was on the CVL 23, the *USS Princeton*. As later groups were formed and rotation was started, the sequence was altered.

Still another adaptation was to convert smaller mercantile hulls to auxiliary carriers. These were regarded as general force multipliers and also for aircrew training and aircraft transport.

The first of these escort carriers was the AVG 1, the *USS Long Island*, commissioned in June 1941, and a conversion of an existing C-3 merchant ship. This was followed by 11 CVEs of the Bogue class. The *USS Bogue* CVE 9 was commissioned in June 1942 and through April 1943 was followed by the *Altamaha, Barnes, Block Island, Breton, Card, Copahee, Core, Croatan, Nassau* and *Prince William*. All of these were built by the Seattle-Tacoma Shipbuilding Company. Of special interest for this book are two of the CVEs. Gil and Airgroup 27 did their carrier qualification on the CVE *Copahee* in San Francisco Bay and were transported from Alameda to Hawaii on the CVE *Barnes*.

Next, came four Sangamon class CVEs:

| | |
|---|---|
| *USS Sangamon* (class) | commissioned August 1942 Newport News |
| *USS Chenango* | commissioned September 1942 Norfolk Navy Yard |
| *USS Santee* | commissioned August 1942 Puget Sound Navy Yard |
| *USS Suwannee* | commissioned September 1942 Bethlehem Steel Staten Island, New York |

By far the largest number of CVEs were the 51 Casablanca class carriers, from July 1943-December 1944. These alphabetically were: *Admiralty Islands, Anzio, Attu, Bismark Sea, Bouganville, Cape Esperance, Casablanca, Corregidor, Fanshaw Bay, Gambier Bay, Guadalcanal,*

*Hoggatt Bay, Hollandia, Kadashan Bay, Kalinin Bay, Kasaan Bay, Kitkun Bay, Kwajalein, Liscombe Bay, Longa Point, Makassar Strait, Makin Island, Manila Bay, Marcos Island, Matanikau, Mission Bay, Munda, Natoma Bay, Nehenta Bay, Ommaney Bay, Petrof Bay, Roi, Rudyerd Bay, Saginaw Bay, Salamaua, Sargent Bay, Save Island, Shamrock Bay, Shipley Bay, Sitkah Bay, Solomans, St. Lo, Steamer Bay, Takanis Bay, Thetis Bay, Tripoli, Tulagi, Wake Island, White Plains* and *Windham Bay*. All 51 were built by Kaiser Shipbuilding Company, Vancouver, Washington.

The final group of CVLs was the *Commencement Bay* class. Nineteen of them were commissioned in 1944-45 ; all were built by Todd Shipyards (Tacoma, Portland or Willamette). These alphabetically were: *Badoeng Strait, Bairoko, Block Island, Cape Gloucester, Commencement Bay, Gilbert Islands, Kulo Gulf, Mindoro, Palau, Point Cruz, Puget Sound, Raboul, Rendova, Saidor, Salerno Bay, Siboney, Sicily, Tinian,* and *Vetta Gulf.*

Summary of WWII US Navy Aircraft Carriers

| | | |
|---|---|---|
| Pre-WWII | CV | 7 |
| Essex | class CV | 24 |
| Independence | class CVL | 9 |
| Long Island | class AVG | 1 |
| Bogue | class CVE | 11 |
| Sangamon | class CVE | 4 |
| Casa Blanca | class CVE | 51 |
| Commencement Bay | class CVE | 19 |
| Subtotal | | 126 |
| Late Midway | class CV | 3 |
| Total | | 129 |

During the long history of the United States Navy, there have been six vessels that proudly bore the title *USS Princeton*. "Our" CVL-23 was the fourth, with three going before it and two following.

The first vessel was the Navy's first steam-powered screw-propelled warship launched in September 1843 at the Philadelphia Navy Yard. It was 164' long, 3 masted and with a crew of 166. It was deactivated in June 1849 and eventually scrapped.

The second ship was 177' long and built at the Boston Navy Yard in early 1852. In 1866 it was ordered sold.

112 — THREE FLAGS & TWO BROTHERS

Number three was a composite gunboat, laid down in May 1896 in Philadelphia. It saw action in the Spanish-American War and the Boxer Rebellion. It was decommissioned in June 1903 and recommissioned May 1905. Again decommissioned March 1907, and it was recommissioned in 1909 and finally decommissioned and sold in 1919.

The CVL-23 *USS Princeton,* the fourth, was laid down as the Cruiser Tallahassee CL, but before completion a flight deck was added and it became an Independence class light carrier. It served from February 1943 until sinking October 24, 1944.

The fifth ship was an Essex class large carrier, the *USS Princeton* CV-37, from 1946 until sometime in the 1980s.

The sixth, and last, ship was an Aegis cruiser, the *USS Princeton* CG-59, from 1988 to the present.

The Independence class light aircraft carrier (CVL) carried an air group. These consisted of one squadron of F6F Grumman Hellcat fighter planes and one squadron of Grumman Avenger TBM torpedo bombers, which is what Gil flew on. Besides use as a torpedo bomber, the Avenger served as a horizontal bomber, night bomber, reconnaissance and anti-submarine aircraft.

GRUMMAN TBF-1 AVENGER DROPPING A TORPEDO
(USN - U.S. NAVY NAVAL AVIATION NEWS 15 FEBRUARY 1944)

The TBF/M Avenger was the biggest single engine aircraft during WWII. She was first ordered into production in December 1940 with the first delivery just in time for the battle of Midway. The Avenger was characterized by its rigid and strong body and its versatilities.

HOLLY'S SCALE MODEL OF THE AVENGER

**TBF/M Avenger Specifications and Characteristics**

Manufacturer: General Motors Corporation Eastern Aircraft Division Trenton, NJ

Crew: 3 pilot, gunner, radio operator/bombardier/navigator combination

Length: 40' 11 ½"

Wing Span: 54' 2"

Wing Area: 490 sq. ft.

Height: 16' 5" (one source shows 15' 5")

Weight: Empty 10,545 lbs.

Weight: Loaded 17, 893 lbs.

Power: 1 Wright R2600 (20 piston radial engine) 1900 HP

Speed: Max 276 MPH at 16,500 ft.

Speed: Cruise 147 MPH

Ceiling: 30,000 ft.

Range: 1,010 miles

Climb Rate: 2,060 ft/min.

Wing Loading: 36.5 ft lb2

Power/Mass: . 0094 HP/lb.

Armament: 1 30-caliber nose-mounted machine gun
           2 50-caliber wing-mounted machine gun
           1 50-caliber dorsal-mounted machine gun
           1 30-caliber ventral-mounted machine gun
           1 2,000 lb. torpedo or up to 2,000 lb. of bombs

The wings of the Avenger were designed to fold back laterally along the fuselage, to alleviate the height problem caused on carrier hanger decks by upward-folded wings. The hydraulically powered wings could be folded or unfolded by the pilots in seconds and required no assistance from hanger deck crews.

The record month for TBM production was March 1945 when Eastern built 400 aircraft in 30 days.

Avenger became the Navy's standard and most effective torpedo bomber during WWII, but it could deliver other payloads as well. Armed with depth charges in the Atlantic, Avenger played a key role in defeating German U-boats. In the Pacific, Avengers struck targets on both land and sea. Teamed with dive bombers, Avengers helped sink the Japanese *Yamato* and other large ships.

GRUMMAN F6F-3 HELLCAT IN TRICOLOR CAMOFLAGE
(U.S. NAVY NATIONAL MUSEUM OF NAVAL AVIATION MAY 1943)

Air Group 27 consisted of two squadrons. Torpedo Bomber Squadron 27 had 18 Avengers, nine configured as bombers and nine configured as torpedo bombers. Fighter Squadron 27 had 12 Grumman F6F Hellcats.

The Hellcat was designed to be easy to manufacture, maintain and fly. It was in large scale production from October 1942 until war's end with 12,274 being built.

## Hellcat Specifications and Characteristics

Wingspan: 42'10"
Length: 33'7"
Power: 2,000 HP R2800 10W double Wasp engine
Speed: Top 386 MPH
Climb Rate: 3,410 ft./min.
Range: 1,040 miles
Armament: 6 50-caliber machine guns with 2,400 rounds of ammo
      2,000 lb. bombs
      6 5-inch rockets

HOLLY'S SCALE MODEL OF THE HELLCAT

11 May 1945, while supporting the invasion of Okinawa, aircraft carrier USS Bunker Hill burns after being hit by two kamikaze planes within 30 seconds.
(U.S. Navy- National Archives)

Japanese battleship Yamato blows up, following massive attacks by U.S. Navy carrier planes north of Okinawa, 7 April 1945. An escorting destroyer is at left. Photographed from a USS Yorktown (CV-10) plane.
(U.S. Naval Historical Center—Collection of Fleet Admiral Chester W. Nimitz)

# 11

## GILBERT REES, NAVY 1942-1949

*"I know that Gil had a life jacket and was in the water for several hours, but I don't know what time he left the USS Princeton or which ship picked him up. He was one of the 1,400-plus survivors of the sinking. He told me that they wanted to give him a Purple Heart but that since he was not wounded, he declined to accept it."*

**IN MANY WAYS, THE NAVY YEARS WERE THE BEST** in Gilbert E. Rees, Jr.'s short life. Before he got interested in radio and ham radio, he was not focused or motivated. This area of interest led him into a successful period of Navy service. Following his discharge and divorce, he again seemed to drift and wander without focus.

Gil served in the U.S. Navy for seven years and two days, spanning parts of eight calendar years. I will now walk us through, in chronological order, the main events and happenings of his Navy years.

During the spring of 1942 he was in contact with the Navy recruiters to complete the process to enroll in the Navy's "V-6" program. This would enable him to enlist as a seaman first class and be assured of training and assignment in the Navy air radio and/or radar work.

Our parents were not too keen on him enlisting but agreed for him to enlist after he turned 18 on July 24, 1942. High school graduation was on June 2, 1942, and all the pieces were lining up for his enlistment. Among the many papers in his records is a form signed by our father since he was under 21 years of age (18). I always thought that it was strange and inconsistent that Dad had to sign for Gil to go into the Navy at 18 but did not have to sign for me to be drafted into the Army. The prospects of becoming a fatality or causality were much higher for me than for Gil.

Gil enlisted in the U.S. Naval Reserve "V-6" as a Seaman 1st Class at Phoenix, Arizona, on August 18, 1942. He went by bus to San Diego, California, and was in boot camp there from August 19 to September 23, 1942.

A roster of C. 42-465 at the Naval Training Station shows 157 sailors in his group. These men came from 16 states as follows: California 64; Colorado 23; Iowa 18; Louisiana 11; New Mexico 10; Arizona 9; Texas 6; Missouri 4; Illinois and Mississippi: 3 each: and 1 each from Alabama, Kentucky, Maryland, New Jersey, Oklahoma, and Washington.

Next it was a troop train from San Diego to Houston, Texas, September 23-25, 1942. My parents and I drove down from Prescott to Phoenix to see Gil briefly as the troop train made a short stop in Phoenix. I can still remember how hot and dirty it was at the train station in Phoenix!

COMMUNICATIONS SCHOOL GROUP "E" UNIVERSITY OF HOUSTON, 1942

GRADUATION CERTIFICATE, RADIO COMMUNICATIONS SCHOOL, UNIVERSITY OF HOUSTON, DEC. 1942

From September 26 to December 22, 1942, Gil was enrolled in a three-month training program at the University of Houston.

His graduation certificate shows: "Elementary Electricity and Radio Materiel." At this time, December 22, 1942, he was promoted from Seaman 1st Class to Radio Technician 3rd Class and given five days' leave.

 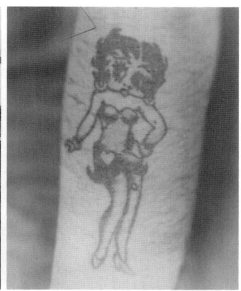

1942. University of Houston      Gil's Betty Boop Tatoo

When he came to Prescott, we found out he had met Dorothy Wagner in Houston and sported a large tattoo of Betty Boop on his left forearm. Here are pictures of his University of Houston class (Gil is top row, far left) and a picture of his tattoo (which greatly upset our mother). Gil later had tattoo remorse and tried to have the tattoo removed, which resulted in a lot of ugly scarring.

Following his brief leave, Gil reported to the Naval Training Station at Corpus Christi, Texas, on December 27, 1942, for seven months of training at Ward Island on Aviation Radio Materiel.

Gil's records show that from December 29, 1942 to January 25, 1943, he was a patient at the U.S. Navy Hospital in Corpus Christi, TX. I have no recollection, and can find nothing in his records as to why.

On February 16, 1943, he completed a course and qualified on Aviation Radar. From February 16, 1943, for five months he was enrolled at Ward Island Naval Training Station, Corpus Christi, Texas, in the Aviation Radio Materiel (ARM) program.

August 7, 1943, was the timing for three events: (1) promotion to Aviation Radio Technician 2nd Class, (2) a certificate in Special Aviation Radio Equipment USN, and (3) Aircraft Engine Mechanics, Corpus Christi Junior College.

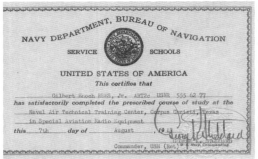

AVIATION RADIO CERTIFICATE, CORPUS CHRISTI, 1943

PETTY OFFICER 2ND CLASS UNIFORM

September 1, 1943, he was transferred to Fleet Air at the Naval Air Station, Alameda, California, in CASU 6 (carrier air service unit) "for CASU 18 when ready." September 23 to November 1, 1943, he was a shop tech in CASU 18 at an auxiliary field at Watsonville, California. From November 1, 1943, to March 6, 1944, he was in CASU 37 at another auxiliary field at Hollister, California.

On March 6, 1944, Gil was assigned to Torpedo Squadron 27 in Air Group 27 (this also included Fighter Squadron 27) and designated as "CAC" (combat air crew). He would remain assigned to VT 27 until August 17, 1945.

I am going to walk us through this 17 plus months of action on the *USS Princeton* CVL 23 and *USS Independence* CVL 22 mostly from Gil's records. For a more complete and detailed coverage, I recommend reading W. H. Buracker's article in the *National Geographic* magazine and Bradshaw and Clark's *Carrier Down*.

On March 6, 1944, Gil was promoted to Aviation Radio Technician 1st Class. The Air Group 27 received carrier qualification on the CVE *Copahee* in San Francisco Bay, then back to NAS Alameda, California, and on March 22, 1944, boarded the CVE *Barnes*. Air Group 27 on the *Barnes* left the continental U.S. on March 23, 1944, bound for Hawaii.

The air group was to receive training on the island of Maui (at auxiliary fields Kahului and Puonene) until the *USS Princeton* CVL 23 returned from Seattle. On April 1, 1944, Gil completed training and received a certificate of qualification for ART 1 and ACRT.

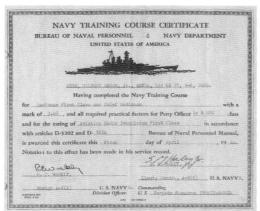

1ST CLASS/CHIEF PETTY OFFICER
AVIATION RADIO CERTIFICATE

Gil had a group picture of Air Group 27 taken on April 20, 1944, on Maui and another of Torpedo Squadron 27 the same day. In this picture, Gil is second from the right: third is Daniel H. Forsythe, gunner on his crew; and fourth is Lt. John G. Dooling, the pilot. This crew of three would serve together for the remainder of the war.

In early May the air group had a joint exercise with both the fighter and bomber squadrons participating.

AIR GROUP 27, MAUI, HAWII, 1944

On May 14 the air group returned to Ford Island at Pearl Harbor and boarded the CVL 23 *USS Princeton*. On May 15th the *USS Princeton* sailed out for a two-day exercise with the *USS Yorktown* and *USS Langley* and returned to Pearl Harbor for nine days of repair and to receive a battle paint job.

On May 29th the *USS Princeton* left Pearl Harbor to join Task Force 58 at Mojuro. On June 2nd they crossed the 180th Meridian, and Gil became a citizen of the Domain of the Golden Dragon. On June 6th he was designated as Combat Air Crewman qualifying on the TBH-1 (Grumman Avenger).

June 13 to July 28 they were engaged in the Marianas Islands campaign. For this action Gil received his first Air Medal (see citation below). There were 15 carriers in Task Force 58, and they were involved in the "Great Marianas Turkey Shoot."

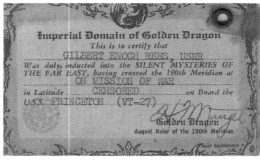

180TH MERIDIAN CERTIFICATE

THE SECRETARY OF THE NAVY
WASHINGTON

The President of the United States takes pleasure in presenting the AIR MEDAL to

GILBERT ENOCH REES, JR.
AVIATION CHIEF ELECTRONICS TECHNICIAN'S MATE
UNITED STATES NAVY

for service as set forth in the following

CITATION:

"For meritorious achievement in aerial flight as Aircrewman of a Navy Torpedo Plane in Torpedo Squadron TWENTY SEVEN, attached to the U.S.S. PRINCETON, during sustained operations against enemy Japanese forces in the Marianas Islands, from June 13 to July 28, 1944. Participating in numerous successful bombing attacks on enemy airfields, defenses and installations, and in several missions in support of our ground troops, REES rendered invaluable assistance to his pilot in carrying out these missions. His technical skill and devotion to duty reflect the highest credit upon REES and the United States Naval Service."

For the President,

*James Forrestal*

Secretary of the Navy

SEC. NAVY, CITATION FOR GIL'S FIRST AIR MEDAL

Following the Marianas action, the task force moved to the Western Carolines for the Palaus and specifically Peleliu.

On September 1st they crossed the equator at latitude 00"00' and longitude 155° 11'E and joined the Domain of Neptune Rex. Later they did some preliminary strikes in the Philippines and returned to Ulithi. In early October they rode out a typhoon while moored at Ulithi. Later there were strikes on Okinawa and Formosa and on October 21st they flew photo missions over Luzon.

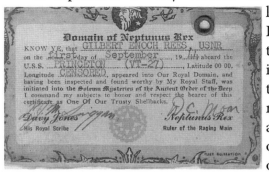

INTERNATIONAL DATELINE CERTIFICATE

Admiral W. F. Halsey's third fleet consisted of eight large carriers, eight light carriers, six battleships, 15 cruisers and 58 destroyers. One of four task groups that included the *USS Princeton* also included large carrier *USS Essex* and *USS Lexington,* sister CVL *USS Langley,* battleships *USS South Dakota* and *USS Massachusetts,* cruisers *USS Mobile, USS Birmingham, USS Santa Fe* and *USS Reno* and 13 destroyers.

In the early hours of October 24, 1944, before first light, the Princeton had fighters in the air flying patrol and reconnaissance to help protect the ships of the Third Fleet and locate the Japanese armada that was known to be approaching.

Then at 9:38 a.m. a lone Japanese plane came in low at less than 1,200 feet and dropped a 500-pound bomb on the *USS Princeton*. It hit forward of the rear elevator and a little to the left of the center of the ship. The bomb penetrated the flight deck and the hanger deck and exploded on the second deck with major damage. The most serious problems on a carrier are the fuel and ammunition in storage, and on the planes that were vulnerable to the flames from the bomb explosion.

The first major explosion occurred at 10:02 a.m. and thus began an eight-hour effort to save the *USS Princeton*. The carrier slowed down from 24 knots to 17-18 knots to finally being dead in the water.

Standing by to assist the *USS Princeton* in fire control and receiving the crew were two cruisers, the *USS Birmingham* CL 62 and Reno CL 96. The *USS Birmingham* was often alongside and suffered more casualties than the *USS Princeton*. The *USS Princeton* had 108 killed and 201 wounded for a total of 309 casualties. The *USS Birmingham* had 241 killed and 412 wounded for a total of 653 casualties.

### USS Princeton on fire east of Luzon, 24 October 1944

The U.S. Navy light aircraft carrier USS Princeton (CVL-23) burning soon after she was hit by a Japanese bomb while operating off the Philippines on 24 October 1944. This view, taken from the battleship USS South Dakota (BB-57) at about 1000 hrs. shows the large smoke column passing aft following a heavy explosion in the carrier's hangar deck

(U.S. Navy–Naval History and Heritage Command)

Also assisting were four destroyers: the *Cassin Young* DD 793, the *Gatling* DD 611, the *Irwin* DD 794 and the *Morrison* DD 560.

Around midday things appeared to be under control and that the rescue efforts were winning. At 3:23 p.m. the worst explosion took place and blew the stern off the *USS Princeton* and caused most of the *USS Birmingham's* casualties. At 4:40 p.m. Capt. Buracker was the last one to leave the *USS Princeton*. Then the destroyer *Irwin* was instructed to fire a torpedo and sink the *Princeton*.

USS BIRMINGHAM (CL-62) COMES ALONGSIDE THE
BURNING USS PRINCETON (CVL-23) TO ASSIST WITH
FIRE FIGHTING, 24 OCTOBER 1944.
(U.S. NAVY–NATIONAL ARCHIVES)

I highly recommend the *Carrier Down* for a detailed account of this entire ordeal with many interviews with the participants.

I know that Gil had a life jacket and was in the water for several hours, but I don't know what time he left the *USS Princeton* or which ship picked him up. He was one of the 1,400-plus survivors of the sinking. He told me that they wanted to give him a Purple Heart but that since he was not wounded, he declined to accept it. I also know that he returned to the states on the battleship BB48 the *West Virginia*.

On November 11th Gil was given the authority to wear Aircrew Wings with three stars. He reentered the continental United States on November 24, 1944, and went to the Alameda Naval Air Station. He left Alameda on December 7th and had 30 days leave plus travel time.

2 July 1946

MEMORANDUM FOR ENLISTED PERSONNEL ATTACHED TO CVLAG-27
DURING THE PERIOD 28 MAY 1944 to 24 OCTOBER 1944.

Dear AG-27ers:

    Attached to this memorandum you will find a letter of commendation from Captain William H. Buracker. This letter was intended for you all when we were detached from the "Princeton" detail in November of 1944. However, as you were well aware, the number of things that had to be done and the limitations of facilities prevented the completion of certain items. Captain Buracker is extremely anxious that each man who was in the Princeton Air Group have a copy of this letter as it commemorates in some sense a memorable period of operations and a job that was well done by each and every one of you. Those of you who are still in the service or in reserve organizations should have this letter included in your personnel records.

    I have managed to keep in touch with a large number of you, but I would like to hear from every one of the old gang. I hope you are all well and enjoying good fortune. If you pass through this area, be sure and drop in to see me.

Sincerely,

F. A. BARDSHAR
Commander, USN

COMMENDATION LETTER 2ND JULY 1946

U.S.S. PRINCETON (CVL-23)

Care of Fleet Post Office,
San Francisco, California.

11 November 1944.

From: The Commanding Officer.
To: REES, Gilbert Enoch, 555 62 77, ART1c, V-6, USNR.

Subject: Commendation.

1. The meritorious conduct which you displayed while serving in the PRINCETON, during the period from 11 June 1944 to the sinking of the ship on 24 October 1944, as a result of enemy action, is deserving of special recognition. During this period, the PRINCETON participated in all major engagements which took place in the Western Pacific, and at the time of her sinking was engaged in offensive operations against the enemy off the east coast of Luzon in the Philippine Islands.

2. During the entire period, the excellent record of the ship and the attached air group was the result of the willing and untiring cooperation of all hands. The remarkably small loss of life when the ship was lost was in itself ample testimony of the high state of morale and discipline which existed on board. I am convinced that your personal loyalty and devotion to duty, in spite of long hard hours of work, on many difficult and dangerous missions, were a material contribution to the PRINCETON's fine record. Therefore, I extend to you my deep appreciation for your fine service, and commend you for a job that was truly well done.

3. A copy of this letter will be attached to your record.

W. H. BURACKER.

**COMMENDATION LETTER 11 NOVEMBER 1944**

Gil married Dorothy Wagner in Houston, Texas, on December 18th and reported for duty in Sanford, Maine on January 14, 1945. I remember him commenting on the culture and climate shock of going to New England in January after being in the South Pacific, California, and Texas.

GIL AND DOROTHY, 1946

On March 1st Gil was promoted from ART 1st Cl. to ACRT (AA)(T)— Aviation Chief Radio Technician.

Then it was back south and a return to Ward Island at the Naval Air Station, Corpus Christi, Texas, on April 10th. He received 10 days leave from April 25 to May 1, 1945. On May 7th he left the continental U.S. to be out of country until August 17, 1945.

Again it was back to Hilo, Hawaii, with Torpedo Squadron 27. The picture of him in his flight gear was taken in Hilo in May 1945.

GIL IN FLIGHT GEAR, 1945

He wore a yellow life belt, parachute, radio helmet, ammunition belt and carried a revolver and Bowie knife.

On June 17th VT 27 left Hawaii on the CVL 22 *USS Independence*, with the Third Fleet. During the period July 10 to August 9, they were engaged in strikes on the Japanese mainland. It was for this series of missions that Gil received his second Air Medal (see citation 2). (Note, also, a picture of a Japanese DE that they sank on July 15th)

On July 24, 1945, Gil celebrated his 21st birthday on his 21st combat mission against the Japanese naval base at Kure. He went on 5 more missions for a total of 26. On August 17th they returned to the continental U.S.

On August 18, 1945, he received his first Good Conduct Medal and was discharged from the U.S. Naval Reserve (Discharge) for the purpose of enlisting in the regular Navy. On August 19th, at Wilmington, California, he was sworn in for a four-year hitch in the United States Navy. His chief's status was made permanent.

From August 19th to October 16th he was assigned to the Naval Air Station in San Diego still with Torpedo Squadron 27. His daughter, Yvonne Ernestine Rees, was born October 11, 1945, in Glendale, California. (With Uncle Holly, on leave standing in for absent father Gil!) Finally Gil got 60 days' leave from October 16th to December 15th. He reported back to San Diego for assignment. During this time he filed a claim for reimbursement for personal property he lost in the sinking of the *Princeton*.

> THE SECRETARY OF THE NAVY
> WASHINGTON
>
> The President of the United States takes pleasure in presenting the GOLD STAR in lieu of a Second Air Medal to
>
> GILBERT ENOCH REES, JUNIOR
> AVIATION CHIEF ELECTRONIC TECHNICIAN'S MATE
> UNITED STATES NAVY
>
> for service as set forth in the following
>
> CITATION:
>
> "For meritorious achievement in aerial flight as an Aircrewman in a Torpedo Bomber in Torpedo Squadron TWENTY SEVEN, attached to the U.S.S. INDEPENDENCE, during operations against enemy forces in the vicinity of the Japanese Homeland from July 10 to August 9, 1945. Completing his fifth combat mission during this period, REES contributed to the success of his plane in the infliction of damage and destruction on enemy shipping, airfields and military installations. His devotion to duty in the face of enemy antiaircraft fire was in keeping with the highest traditions of the United States Naval Service."
>
> For the President,
>
> *John L. Sullivan*
> Secretary of the Navy

## GIL'S GOLD STAR CITATION, 1945

On January 30, 1946, he reported to the Naval Training Center Great Lakes in HEDRON 14-2 FAW 14 for temporary duty as an EE & RM student. In February he took 10 days' leave and April 21 reported back to the Naval Air Training Center Corpus Christi, Texas, as an instructor in airborne electrical maintenance.

I had originally thought the picture of Gil and his wife Dorothy (pge. 132) was a wedding picture, but he is wearing a chief's uniform in the image, so I think this picture was later since he didn't make chief until well after they were married.

JAPANESE DESTROYER ESCORT DESTROYED BY GIL'S CREW, USS INDEPENDENCE TORPEDO SQUADRON 27, JULY 15, 1945

GIL'S PRIVATE PILOT CERTIFICATE, JANUARY 1949

Later, December 20, 1946, to January 6, 1947, he took 16 days' leave. While in Corpus Christi Gil took flying lessons. On May 20, 1947, he qualified on the aircraft engine exam. On June 7, 1947, he received a graduation certificate from the American Aviator Activities and his private pilot license. I think he took this pilot training, which was covered by the VA, under the GI Bill. He also participated in the Civil Air Patrol during this assignment.

From October 15, 1947, to March 8, 1949, he was assigned to the Naval Air Training Center in Memphis, Tennessee. On August 18, 1949, he was awarded his second Good Conduct Medal.

NAVAL AIR STATION, JACKSONVILLE, FLORIDA 1949

TRAINING AIRCRAFT

His records show that he was in the hospital at the NATC Memphis from February 23, 1949, until March 8, 1949 as "patient in Hospital for Treatment." Just like his previous hospitalization, I don't have a clue what it was for. He had a CAA medical certificate for private pilot at the NATC Memphis dated January, 5, 1949. He took 10 days' of leave prior to reporting for his next assignment March 31 to April 11, 1949.

On April 18, 1949, he reported to the Naval Air Station at Jacksonville, Florida, in FASRON 6, where he remained until August 12 when he was transferred to the separation center there.

He received his second discharge this time from the regular Navy on August 19, 1949. This completed his Navy career after seven years and two days. He had four years and six days in the U.S. Navy (regular) and three years and a day in the U.S. Naval Reserves.

## Torpedo Squadron 27 Missions, July 1945

No. 1. 10 July 1945: Aircraft and Installations, Kasumigaura Airfield, Honshu, Japan.

No. 2. 10 July 1945: Aircraft and Installations, Konoike Airfield, Honshu, Japan.

No. 3. 14 July 1945: Shipping off Southern Hokkaido, Japan.

No. 4. 14 July 1945: Naval and Merchant Shipping, Muroran, Hokkaido, Japan.

No. 5. 15 July 1945: Merchant Shipping in vicinity of Hakodate, Hokkaido, Japan.

No. 6. 18 July 1945: Battleship Nagato, Yokosuka Naval Base, Honshu, Japan.

No. 7. 24 July 1945: Naval Shipping at Kure Naval Base, Honshu, Japan. (Oyoda).

No. 8. 24 July 1945: Naval Shipping at Kure Naval Base, Honshu, Japan. (Tone).

No. 9. 25 July 1945: Ground Installations and Shipping, Heki, Honshu, Japan.

Memos:

No. 1. _____

No. 2. _____

No. 3. _____

No. 4. _____

## Torpedo Squadron 27
## Plan of the Day, July 30, 1945

```
                TORPEDO SQUADRON TWENTY SEVEN

                       PLAN OF THE DAY

                           MONDAY

                       30 J U L Y 1945

DUTY OFFICER:   0000-1200   Lieut. GANNON       Rm. 0215   Ph. 952
                Standby     Lieut. FROST            216
                1200-2400   Lieut. ALEXANDER        0215       952
                Standby     Lt(jg) AYMAR            304        906

0700            FLIGHT QUARTERS.

0800 - 1200     STRIKE E-3.

                STALNAKER    HAYES-GUZMAN         T-30    31 Locust
                BERARDINELLI NAGY-GIBSON          T-38    3416    "
                MYER         KELLNER-JOHNSON      T-36    3417    "

                GANNON       DICKSON-EVANS        T-31    3420    "
                COLE         BOTTOMLEY-LYNCH      T-37    3421    "
                WALTERS      CHASTIN-LINDSTROM    T-34    3418    "

                STREET       JOHNSON-CHAMBERLAIN  T-32    3422    "
                STAUBER      LAPIERRE-MARTZ       T-35    3423    "
                ANDERSON     FRANCIS-WOLFF        T-33    3408    "

1230            FLIGHT QUARTERS.

1330 - 1730     STRIKE E-6.

                DOOLING      FORSYTHE-REES        T-30    6401    "
                WILSON       MILLISTEFR-JORDAN    T-38    6406    "
                ROGERS       HARRINGTON-HARDISON  T-35    6407    "

                SAMPLE       PEARSON-KISSELL      T-36    6412    "
                HERVEY       LYNCH-BOEH           T-37    6413    "
                BROWN        FITCH-DOLAN          T-32    6411    "

                GANNON       DICKSON-EVANS        T-31    6420    "
                ALEXANDER    ANDERSON-KING        T-34    6410    "
                ANDERSON     SHEPHERD-ALLEN       T-33    6408    "

Submitted:  J. V. AYMAR,         Approved:  J. G. DOOLING,
            Lt(jg), USNR,                   Lieut., USNR,
            Schedules.                      Commanding.
```

# GILBERT ENOCH REES, JR.
## Service History

Medals and Decorations:

Navy Aircrew Wings with three stars
   Aviation Chief Electronics Technician
      Combat Air Crew

Air Medal with one gold star for second award
   1. 13 June 1944 to 28 July 1944
   2. 10 July 1945 to 9 August 1945

Good Conduct Medal with Second Award bar
   1. August 18, 1945
   2. August 18, 1948

Asiatic Pacific Theater Metal with 4 bronze battle stars
   1. Marianas
   2. Western Caroline Islands
   3. Leyte Operations
   4. 3rd Fleet operations against Japan

American Theater Medal

WWII Victory Medal

Occupation Medal

Philippine Liberation Medal with one bronze star

Gilbert Enoch Rees, Jr. United States Navy

August 18, 1942 to August 19, 1949

Rank and Ratings Held

| | |
|---|---|
| Seaman 1st Class | 8-18-42 |
| Radio Technician 3rd Class | 12-22-42 |
| Aviation Radio Tech. 2nd Class | 8-7-43 |
| Aviation Radio Tech. 1st Class | 3-6-44 |
| Aviation Chief Radio Tech. | 3-1-45 (Temp.) |
| Aviation Chief Radio Tech. | 8-19-45 (Perm.) |
| Aviation Chief Electronic Tech. Mate | 10-7-47 |
| Aviation Technician Chief | 4-2-48 |

**SUMMARY—Itinerary—Assignments for Gilbert**

| From | To | What | Where |
|---|---|---|---|
| | 8-18-42 | Induction Center | Phoenix, AZ |
| 8-19-42 | 9-23-42 | Naval Training Station | San Diego, CA |
| 9-23-42 | 9-25-42 | Troop Train | |
| 9-26-42 | 12-22-42 | EE & RM School, University of Houston | Houston, TX |
| 12-22-42 | 12-27-42 | Delay in route | Prescott, AZ |
| 12-27-42 | 8- -43 | NTS ARM | Corpus Christi, TX |
| 9-1-43 | 9-22-43 | Fleet Air NAS CASU 6 | Alameda CA |
| 9-23-43 | 11-1-43 | CASU 18 | Watsonville, CA |
| 11-1-43 | 3-6-44 | CASU 37 | Hollister, CA |
| 3-6-44 | 3-17-45 | Torpedo Squadron 27 | Alameda, CA |
| 3-22-44 | | *CVE Barnes* | Alameda to Maui, |
| | 5- -45 | NATS | Maui, HI |
| 5-14- 44 | 10-24-44 | *CVL Princeton* | Various |
| | 10-24-44 | *CVL Princeton* sunk by the Japs | Leyte Gulf |
| | 11-24-44 | *BB-48 West Virginia* | Return to USA |
| 12-7-44 | 1-14-45 | leave, Marriage | NAS Alameda, CA |
| 1-14-45 | 4-10-45 | NAS Sanford, ME | *BB-48 West Virginia* |
| 4-10-45 | 4-25-45 | NAS | Corpus Christi, TX |
| 4-26-45 | 5-1-45 | 10 days leave | |
| 5-7-45 | 6-19-45 | Leave cont. US | Arrive Hilo, HI |
| 6-17-45 | 8-17-45 | *CVL Independence* | Various |

| From | To | What | Where |
|---|---|---|---|
| 08-18-45 | 08-19-45 | NAS Discharge and re-up | Wilmington, CA |
| 08-14-45 | 10-16-45 | NAS | San Diego, CA |
| 10-16-45 | 12-15-45 | 60 days leave | San Diego, CA |
| 12-15-45 | 01- -46 | NAS | San Diego, CA |
| 01-30-46 | | NATC 10 days leave | Great Lakes, IL |
| 04-21-46 | 10- -46 | NATC | Corpus Christi, TX |
| 12-20-46 | 01-06-47 | 16 days leave | |
| 10-15-47 | 03-30-49 | NATC | Memphis, TN |

| | | | |
|---|---|---|---|
| 03-31-49 | 04-11-49 | 10 days leave | |
| 04-11-49 | 08-12-49 | NAS | Jacksonville, FL |
| 08-12-49 | 08-14-49 | Separation Center Discharge | Jacksonville, FL |

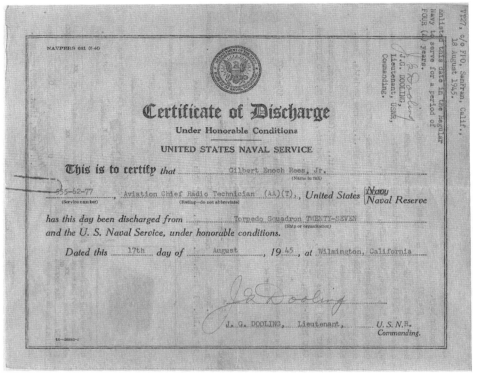

1ST DISCHARGE, GIL'S TRANSFER FROM NAVAL RESERVE TO DIRECT NAVY SERVICE, 1945

CERTIFICATE FOR THE GILBERT REES BRICK SET IN THE "ROAD TO VICTORY" WALKWAY AT THE NATIONAL WWII MUSEUM IN NEW ORLEANS

# COLOR ALBUM

## Keepsakes of War

The Three Flags
Infantry Fatigue Jacket
Infantry Canteen
Infantry Boot
Holly Rees G.I. Dog Tags
Infantry Bayonet
Decommissioned .50 Cal BMG Round
Decommissioned U.S. Fragmentation Grenade
Holly Rees Combat infantry Badge,
Purple Heart, & Bronze Star

## Holly E. Rees, Present Day

### Wearing his WWII Infantry Uniform with Standard Insigina and Decorations

# The Hinomaru Yosegoui —

an individual Japanese silk flag inscribed with personal messages in Kanji characters.

carried by Imperial Japanese Infantryman Tomoe Sanshi, taken by U.S. Infantryman Holly Reese after he killed Tomoe Sanshi in combat during the Okinawa Campaign.

144 — Three Flags & Two Brothers

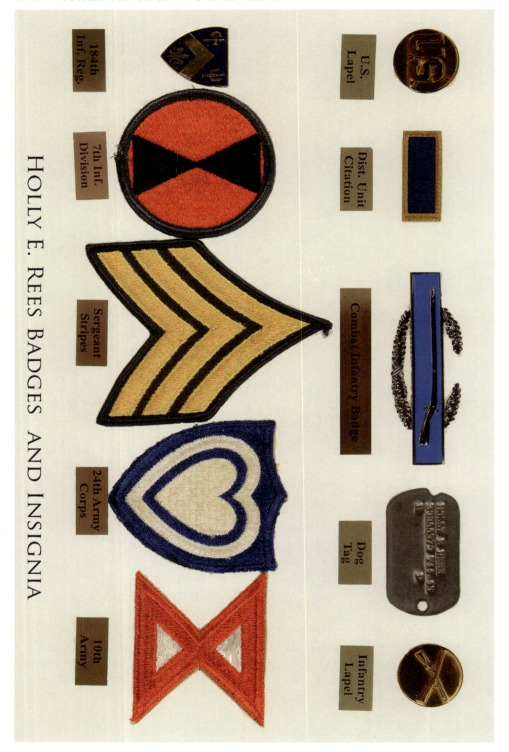

HOLLY E. REES MEDALS

146 — Three Flags & Two Brothers

Gilbert E. Rees Medals

Holly E. Rees landing at Naha, Okinawa

— Okinawa Veterans Return —
(l-r) U.S. Marine Harry Bender, historian and Guide Hugh Ambrose, U.S. Marine R.V. Burgin, U.S. Infantryman Holly E. Rees

View of Udo Village, Okinawa, Modern Day

Outside Mabuni, above Udo Village, Holly Rees stands near the cave from which the Japanese sniper fired the shot that wounded him 62 years before.

## The Golden Pavilion
Kyoto, Japan

## At the Dome in Hiroshima

# Part Three

## Post Military Life

# 12

## Gilbert Rees – Post Navy

*"One of life's many imponderables is that Gil survived 26 combat missions and the sinking of the USS Princeton only to die, needlessly, in a one-car accident. Another "why" is that in July 1952, Betty, Lane, and I walked away from a one-car accident and barely a year later in July 1953 Gil died."*

**Following his discharge from the Navy** (after seven years of service) on August 19, 1949, Gil lived for less than four years in civilian life before his tragic and untimely death. In many ways his time in the Navy was the best time of his life.

From my perspective, his life was without purpose or direction until he got interested in "ham" (amateur) radio in high school. This blossomed and led to his career in the Navy, which also introduced a love for flying to his interest in radio, radar and electronics.

After hostilities ended he stayed in the Navy for four years but afterward, once again seemed to lose focus and direction. He dabbled with a number of activities. During the four years after his discharge, he seemed to drift and lose even more focus and purpose. I will piece together what I can of those years in a more or less chronological order.

Following his discharge, Gil and his family moved back home to Prescott, Arizona where our father had established his automotive machine shop, Rees Motor Rebuild. Fairly early on they bought the Shiminoski house at 201 N. Washington St., which was only a block from our parent's home at 138 No. Virginia Street. Dad's shop was at the back of the lot, behind the house where they lived.

One weekend in October 1949, Gil and Dorothy drove to Phoenix, where I lived and worked, to attend a football game between the University of Arizona and Arizona State University at Tempe. My girlfriend Betty came from Tucson, and we double dated. I don't remember who won the football game, but this was always one arch rivalry. We also attended the Arizona State Fair and had an enjoyable weekend together.

Shortly afterwards Betty came to Prescott to spend Christmas with my parents and me, and this is when we became engaged. Again we were all together, sharing Christmas and our time together.

GIL AND HIS DAUGHTER, YVONNE, 1952

The next month I quit my job in Phoenix and went home to prepare to move to Dallas in anticipation of our wedding in June 1950. I didn't have much money and was trying to see what I could sell (actually, hock is more what I had in mind) to raise some money. Mom and Dad bought my binoculars and Monroe calculator, and Gil bought my 22 rifle and the Arisaka rifle I'd brought home from the war. I have always regretted selling him the Japanese rifle.

I moved to Dallas in February 1950, joined the Methodist Church and found a job with the Firestone Tire and Rubber Company. Since I now had a job, we moved our wedding from June to April 23, 1950.

Neither my parents nor my brother came to our wedding for whatever reason, probably time and distance.

In either late 1949 or early 1950, Gil signed up with the Veterans Administration for vocational training under the GI Bill. The VA bought him a set of hand tools and he was to be an apprentice to my father to learn automotive machine work. I don't know how this progressed, but the arrangement was terminated on November 30, 1950. Correspondence shows that the VA wanted the hand tools returned or paid for. A later determination permitted him to keep them.

Gil had started with the Civil Air Patrol while in the Navy and rejoined as a pilot in Arizona in September 1950 and again in April 1952.

In January 1951 Gil started training to be a fireman with the Atchison Topeka and Santa Fe railroad. His records show that he was still working on this in May 1951 and in July 1951. Correspondence in October 1951 shows that he was not entitled to railroad unemployment benefits. He had joined the Brotherhood of Locomotive Firemen and Engineers on July 25, 1951.

The picture of Gil and Yvonne on the front steps at our parents' home in Prescott is not dated. Gil is wearing a western style belt with silver buckle that I gave him for Christmas in 1949. Yvonne was 7 when Gil died so I am guessing this was about 1952.

I have no idea what it is/was, but I have a card showing that he joined the National Society of Buffalos, Arizona Lodge #2, on June 17, 1951. When our son, Lane was born June 23, 1951, I called to tell my folks, they weren't home and I talked to Gil. I think this was the last time that I talked with him.

The next event was Dorothy filing for divorce. This was Divorce #18421 in Yavapai County District Court. Gil did not appear in the procedure or have representation, and the divorce was finalized on March 4, 1952. The terms provided that Dorothy would get the house and car. She would get custody of daughter Yvonne, he would have reasonable visitation rights and he would pay $50.00 per month for child support.

He joined the Civil Air Patrol, Arizona Wing (an Auxiliary of the U.S. Air Force) on April 11, 1952.

At some point he went to work for Newmont Exploration Ltd. of Jerome, Arizona, and first worked in Royal, New Mexico. I suspect that he was doing this when the divorce proceedings were going on.

Another document dated June 26, 1952, shows that Gil "is a qualified geophysical engineer and member of the geophysical exploration survey party of Newmont Exploration Ltd. He is entering Canada for the purpose of assisting in carrying out a geophysical survey on behalf of Newmont Exploration Ltd. on the property of the Pacific Nickel Co. Ltd. near Yale, B.C.—for approximately 4 months."

The next items on the radar screen were drawing unemployment compensation in November 1952, joining the National Rifle Association in December 1952 and the International Association of Machinists Lodge #933 on December 15, 1952 as an electronic technician.

This was probably about the same time he went to work for Hughes Aircraft in Tucson, Arizona. He had a card showing the Hughes Employees

Give Once Club, dated May 28, 1953. Also a State of Arizona Operator's License #72597 dated May 28, 1953, showing brown hair, blue eyes, 6'0" and 175 lbs.

The next and final chapter in Gil's life occurred in July 2, 1953. He was living and working in Tucson. He and a co-worker at Hughes Aircraft Co., James C. Shepherd, had driven to Nogales. They were on their way back to Tucson when at 3:30 a.m. the 1946 car hurtled off a curve on U.S. 89, 20.2 miles north of Nogales. The car jumped a dry wash and plowed into an embankment, killing both of them instantly. James owned the car, but Gil was driving when the one-car accident happened. One of life's many imponderables is that Gil survived 26 combat missions and the sinking of the USS Princeton only to die, needlessly, in a one-car accident. Another "why" is how, in July 1952, Betty, Lane and I walked away from a one-car accident when barely a year later a similar accident took Gil's life.

Gil and James were the 196th and 197th fatalities on Arizona highways in 1953. The bodies were taken to Carroon Mortuary in Nogales and later Gil's body was sent to Ruffner Funeral Home in Prescott.

Mom called to tell me of Gil's death. Since our daughter, Ann, was just a month old, we decided that Betty would stay in San Angelo with our two

CONDITION OF THE AUTO AFTER THE ACCIDENT
IN WHICH GILBERT REES WAS KILLED, JULY 1953

small children and I would fly out to Prescott for the funeral. I flew out of San Angelo on a small plane to Midland, then to El Paso, on to Phoenix and then another small plane to Prescott.

The 4th of July and the annual "Frontier Days" celebration and rodeo are a big deal in Prescott. Thus, the funeral was delayed for a few days. Also, the annual monsoons were on schedule and it was pouring down rain. The day of the funeral and burial was delayed for another day. Rev. Charles F. Parker of the First Congregational Church officiated at the funeral, and burial was in the family plot at the Mountain View Cemetery.

Dad received the Social Security lump sum death benefit (from Gil's combined railroad retirement, Social Security record) and the Veteran Administration burial allowance and bronze head stone plaque.

Mom was the beneficiary of his National Service (GI) life insurance, and they invested this until Yvonne was 18 and gave the accumulated proceeds to her. I was told by my mother that this lasted only a few months and was blown away in a spending frenzy.

Dorothy filed for survivor's benefits for Yvonne, and she received Social Security monthly benefits until she was 18. Since Dorothy was divorced and remarried, she was not eligible for widow's benefits.

Gil's radio electronics and math books were donated to the Prescott Public Library.

A letter of condolence from Harold L. George, vice president and general manager at Hughes Aircraft Company at Culver City, California, included:

*"May I extend to you my most sincere sympathy. Our company is a young organization. Mr. Rees, with his skill in the new field of electronics, was one of the many young men whose contributions are so important in our effort to make secure the defense of our nation and our way of life. His presence will be missed by his friends with whom he worked."*

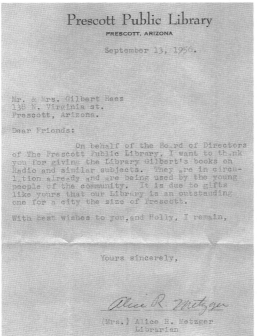

LETTER OF THANKS FROM PRESCOTT PUBLIC LIBRARY, 1956

# 13

## HOLLY REES – POST INFANTRY

*"... well before our first date, another interesting event came up and I called and made a second date, before we had had the first one! My roommate and other friends thought I was off my rocker to make a second date before ever having the first one. We hit it off from the start and it is now 65 years later, which should prove that I knew what I was doing."*

A NEW PHASE IN MY LIFE BEGAN WHEN I RECEIVED my discharge. There were several hours to kill before my train left San Antonio and so I visited the Alamo for the first time. It seemed a shame to live in San Antonio for seven-plus months and not to experience this bastion of Texas history.

My train ticket was to Los Angeles, but I got off in Tucson and rode the bus to Prescott. I remember it was so hot in Tucson that the asphalt felt squishy underfoot. Also, the bus would leave the main highway and go down a country road, and suddenly an Indian would appear and get on the bus. Later, on another tangent, the bus would stop and an Indian would get off. Not a word was spoken, and this routine was repeated several times. I marveled at the system and the apparent lack of conversation.

During my short visit in Prescott a classmate, Daniel R. "Pat" Roe, was flying home from Iceland and the plane crashed, killing all aboard. The pall bearers at his funeral were all members of the class of 1944 at Prescott High School. We wore our uniforms, and it was a very moving and impressive funeral. Before going into the Army I had been a pall bearer for another classmate killed in the war, Raul Berumen. Up until then, all the funerals I had attended were for elderly people, and it was a whole new dimension to bury your peers. All the death and dying in combat seemed surreal, with no funerals or closure.

After my visit in Prescott, I rode the bus to Phoenix and then the train to Los Angeles. My main project for the remainder of the summer was to obtain a car to have while I was in college. I bought a 1937 Ford coupe, basic black and with a 60 horsepower V8 engine. Dad and I (mostly Dad) went over it with a fine tooth comb and rebuilt the engine. I got new seat covers, re-upholstered it and had a good set of wheels to head to college.

I arrived in Tucson in early September 1946, ready to enroll at the University of Arizona. I had lost two years in the Army and was anxious to get on with my life. I took a heavy load of courses every semester and graduated in three years (six semesters) without going to summer school. I made the honor roll all three years and graduated cum laude (with distinction) in June 1949.

When I was discharged, I applied to the Veterans Administration for disability compensation. This was promptly approved, and I was given a permanent 10% service-connected disability rating (which continues to this day). This enabled me to attend college under the Vocational Rehabilitation program rather than the GI Bill, which most of the veterans used. This was more complete, provided longer time, if needed, and a larger monthly check.

I enrolled in the College of Business and Public Administration with a General Business major. One of my first classes was in economic geography, which I liked and aced. After the course was over, Prof. G. F. Herrick gave me a job grading papers for him. Over the next two years I graded papers and was lined up for a few tutoring jobs for the course.

For the entire three years at the University of Arizona, I lived in Yavapai Hall, a men's residence hall on campus. Prof. Herrick and his wife were the resident dorm parents, and I was invited to be a floor monitor, which didn't pay anything but provided free room. I usually

HOLLY IN HIS EISENHOWER JACKET (DYED NAVY BLUE), UA 1947

bought a meal ticket and ate most of my meals at the commons. Some people hated the food there, but after two years in the Army, I didn't think it was that bad—but I enjoyed eating in some of the good restaurants in Tucson for a treat.

After my first year and making the honor roll, I was invited to join Alpha Kappa Psi, honorary business fraternity. I belonged to the Alpha Nu chapter for the rest of the time I was in college. In my senior year I was elected president and later received the Bronze Level/Meritorious Service Award. Our project was to try and get a Bureau of Business Research established at the University of Arizona to help the state in its business growth and development. The effort paid off and, after I left, it was established. The chapter helped pay some of the research costs, and I wrote a thesis on "A Study of Bureaus of Business Research in American Universities in 1949."

During the summer of 1946, besides Prescott and my car project, I belonged to the "52-20" Club (the federally funded unemployment program for veterans—$20 a week for up to 52 weeks).

The summer of 1947 I spent in Prescott, where my parents had moved back by then. I helped my dad convert our garage into an automotive machine shop, Rees Motor Rebuild. We mixed and poured concrete, did carpentry, plumbing and electrical work. We also installed an air compressor, air line, hung tools and anything else needed to get the business going.

The summer of 1948 I got a job at the Treasurer's Office for Yavapai County in the courthouse. This was largely clerical work on the property tax records and filing. On the side I bought a wrecked 1937 Ford station wagon with an 85 horsepower engine. Dad and I rebuilt the engine, and we put it in my coupe (replacing the 60 HP V8). I sanded and taped the outside, and the father of a friend came and spray-painted it a tan color. This Ford coupe, the first car I owned, was affectionately known as "Henry."

One summer, I think it was 1947, a friend of Gil's, Ted Lawhead, invited me to go for an airplane ride with him in a bi-plane. He had his license and I assumed he was a competent pilot. He flew high, low, fast, buzzed a windmill, chased antelope, flew upside down, and tried his best to get me to say "uncle." Having survived the hell of Okinawa, this wasn't so terrifying for me and I forgot about it. A couple of weeks later he took the manager of the Safeway store up for a ride and crashed, killing both of them.

HOLLY, GRADUATION UA 1949

There were lots of veterans at the University of Arizona while I was there. I belonged to a VFW (Veterans of Foreign Wars) post at the university and also the "Bill Bishop Chapter" of the DAV (Disabled American Veterans). My second year I was elected the chapter commander and worked with the town chapter and as our representative to the "Department" (state). My senior year I was elected Department junior vice commander and the next year, Department senior vice commander. I would have been elected Department (Arizona) commander in 1950 had I not resigned to move to Dallas and get married.

As mentioned earlier, I had a job grading papers for economic geography and went to the Business and Public Administration College office to pick up my monthly pittance. During the fall of 1948 they hired a new secretary, who among other jobs, doled out the paychecks. She was a cute, lively blond with a southern accent. Nothing developed until January 1949 when we had the registration for the spring semester. It was held in "Old Main," and she and the paid staff were busy. The Alpha Kappa Psi fraternity (of which I was president) volunteered to help with the registration. When the day was over, I helped her carry stuff back to the BPA office and offered her a ride home. She did not have a car and lived at the YWCA, some six to eight blocks from the university. We stopped by a local gathering place

HOLLY AND BETTY AT THE "Y" IN TUCSON, 1949

where I had a beer and she had a coke. I quickly learned that she didn't "drink" and didn't much approve of anyone else doing so.

A few days later I found out about a Tucson Symphony Orchestra program coming up in a few weeks and I called her up and invited her to go, which she accepted. About a week later, but still well before our first date, another interesting event came up and I called and made a second date, before we had had the first one! My roommate and other friends thought I was off my rocker to make a second date before ever having the first one. We hit it off from the start and it is now 66 years later, which should prove that I knew what I was doing.

# 14

## Family

*"We were married at her home on Sunday afternoon April 23, 1950."*

**After graduating from the University of Arizona,** I took a job and moved to Phoenix. For the next eight months I commuted the 120 miles (one way) nearly every weekend, back to Tucson, to continue my courtship of my southern sweetheart. I was able to stay at Yavapai Hall since there was nearly always an available room. Also, 25 cents per gallon gas helped to make all this driving possible. I probably racked up well over 10,000 miles plus whatever other driving I did.

I would leave from work on Friday afternoon and return late on Sunday night. We spent a lot of time at a small city park near the YWCA. One time there Betty accidently kicked my right foot on the top where I was shot. It hurt like the dickens, but I am sure I made the most of the occasion and this was the first time Betty told me she loved me. That Christmas Betty went to Prescott with me and we got engaged then (1949).

She didn't want to stay in Arizona and I didn't want to live in Mississippi, so we decided on Dallas, Texas, as a compromise in the middle. I quit my job and moved to Dallas to find another. We had planned to marry in June but I got a job in Dallas, so we moved the date up to April 23. We visited stores in Tucson and picked our patterns for china, crystal and silver, and Betty sent them to her mother in Columbia, Mississippi. She promptly threw away our selections and chose new ones for us. I resented this, among other things, but later learned that "our selections were not available in Jackson, Columbia or New Orleans," hence the switch. We did get a lot of nice wedding presents and I came to like the china, silver and crystal we received.

I had arranged for a college buddy in Paducah, Kentucky, to be my best man, but at the last he couldn't make it and so Betty's family provided one. When I drove from Dallas to Columbia to get married, Betty was the only one there I had met. I had never been east of the Mississippi River south of the Mason-Dixon Line and was I in for a culture shock.

We were married at her home on Sunday afternoon April 23, 1950. Our honeymoon consisted of one night at the Nathan Bedford Forest Hotel in downtown Hattiesburg, Mississippi. We spent one day packing wedding presents and drove back to Dallas the next, and I went back to work on Wednesday.

Betty was born Charline Elizabeth Quin on January 11, 1926 (10 days before I was born). She was named for her father, Charles Butler Quin, and her mother, Norflette Elizabeth Collins Quin. She never used these names and always went by Betty or Sister. Her father died when she was 7, and later her mother married Thomas Sylvester Fibich. Betty and her brother, Kenneth, took the last name Fibich, and I knew her as Betty Fibich. When we became 65 and went under Medicare, they required her Medicare card to be Elizabeth F. Rees. At one time nearly all of the legal, formal papers we had had a different combination of names for Betty, but I gradually got some uniformity and consistency. Since she was 10 days older than me, we used to say she was boss for 10 days and I was the rest of the year—but we knew better! This reminds me of the old story of the couple celebrating 60 years of marriage. They were asked the secret of their long marriage. The man said that when they got married they decided that she would make all the small decisions and he would make all the big ones. The interviewer said to him, "That must have been a big responsibility making all the big decisions." "Not really," he replied, "somehow there just haven't been any big decisions."

Our first child, Lane Charles Rees, was born June 23, 1951, in Longview, Gregg County, Texas. He graduated from Stephen F. Austin High School in Bryan, Texas, and earned a bachelor's degree in management and a master's in educational administration from Texas A&M University. He worked for ARCO Alaska for 12 years in human resources, then ARCO International and now owns Human Resources Solutions and lives in Santa Rosa Beach, Florida. He married Brenda Anderson in Bryan on July 1, 1978.

Ann Elizabeth Rees was born May 30, 1953, in San Angelo, Tom Green County, Texas. She also graduated from Stephen F. Austin High in Bryan and earned a B.S. in nursing science from Texas Woman's University in Denton. She married Gary Lynn Davis in Dallas on August 25, 1990. Gary died of cancer in April 2010, and Ann still lives in Albuquerque, New Mexico. Ellen Dale Rees was born August 2, 1954, also in San Angelo.

HOLLY WITH HIS SON, LANE, AND DAUGHTER, ANN, 1953

She graduated in the first graduating class at Bryan High School in 1972 and earned a degree in elementary education from Stephen F. Austin State University in Nacogdoches, Texas. She married Ronald Michael Handberry on July 2, 1977. They live in Shreveport, Louisiana.

All three of our children were born fairly close together, and I knew for years we would have a hard time when they were in college. This covered a seven-year period. We had three years with only one in college, three years when we had two in college and one year when we had all three in college!

HOLLY ESCORTS HIS DAUGHTER, ELLEN, DOWN THE AISLE AT HER WEDDING, ST. PAUL'S METHODIST, BRYAN, TX, JULY 2, 1971

Just after "Year 3," we bought our home and paid cash for it (a long story and we were pretty well spent out).

When we got married we lived in Dallas, Texas, moved first to Tyler, Texas, and then Longview, Texas. This will all be explained under employment. Next it was San Angelo, Texas, Austin, Texas, and finally Bryan, Texas, in May 1957, where we have lived ever since. Even though we moved a lot in our early years, we moved here just before Lane started first grade so the children were able to go through school without moving. We always tried to settle down and enjoy living in each place even though it might not be for very long.

HOLLY AND BETTY'S GRANDCHILDREN (L-R)
BRIAN, LAUREN, CALEB, AND DAVID

Our three children provided us with four grandsons and one granddaughter (Brian, Nathan, David, Caleb, and Lauren). We now have ten great grand-children (Tabbitha, Reese, Leighton, Elizabeth, Ava, Albert, Ellery, Walden, Holly, and Bella).

"The light hadn't gone out yet" (only dimmed some) when the family wanted to celebrate our 50th wedding anniversary in 2000. Betty did very well and we had a good time. I wrote an "acrostic" for the occasion (one of many I have written) and we got some great pictures.

All the children wanted to celebrate our 80th birthdays in January 2006, but Betty had declined a lot more so we had a much smaller, intimate gathering. She did fairly well, and we were all glad for the sharing of love and memories.

FOUR GENERATIONS (L-R):
HOLLY, BRIAN, LEIGHTON, AND LANE

THE REESE FAMILY
AT HOLLY AND BETTY'S 50TH WEDDING ANNIVERSARY, 2000

# Golden Memories 1950 - 2000

**H** ow could Mississippi and Arizona make a connection?
**O** nly by God's grace and with His direction!
**L** eaving family behind, Holly went to Columbia to be wed,
**L** ater, the happy couple started living in Dallas instead.
**Y** es, Firestone & Minneapolis-Honeywell helped pay the bills

**&**

**B** ut then Social Security called with all of its thrills.
**E** ast Texas was next with Tyler and Longview, all green,
**T** hen Lane came along to enlarge the scene.
**T** he next stop was San Angelo - - home for four years,
**Y** ears that were blessed with Ann, Ellen & a tornado with fears.

**R** eceiving another promotion, it was Austin for a while,
**E** ventually being named District Manager in Bryan in style.
**E** ach previous home was for just a short stay,
**S** o forty-three years in Bryan was a whole new way.

**B** ryan Rotary Club has been a regular activity, too,
**I** n addition, St. Paul's U.M.C. has added quite a few.
**G** rand children total five and each one is special to us,
**50** years together and every one a blessed plus!

ACROSTIC POEM, "GOLDEN MEMORIES," CREATED BY HOLLY REES
TO COMMEMORATE 5OTH WEDDING ANNIVERSARY, 2000

Betty and Holly Reese
80th Birthday photo, January 2006

# 15

## Employment to Retirement

*"After I was promoted to district manager (DM) in Bryan, I received a card of congratulation from a former coworker and on it he wrote: "May you always have enough success to keep you happy and enough failure to keep you humble." I still remember this after over 50 years."*

AS SOON AS I RECEIVED MY BSBA, I TOOK A JOB WITH the Arizona Fire Rating Bureau in Phoenix. My title was "policy examiner" and the AFRB was a quasi-governmental entity that reviewed all the fire and extended coverage insurance policies written in Arizona, both residential and commercial. This was a co-op arrangement of the insurance industry and was, so I heard, an attempt to self-regulate and prevent state regulation. The job was a sort of transitional one as many of the examiners moved on to sell/write insurance policies for the agencies around the state (sort of like accountants doing a stint with the IRS).

While I worked there, television came to Arizona. From the north side of our office we could watch them build the antennae on top of the Westward Ho Hotel, which was the tallest building in Phoenix at that time. With the tall antennae on top of the hotel, it gave the TV station broadcast signal a good coverage. One day a fire broke out at the base of the antennae on top of the hotel as we watched excitedly. I could just picture a major catastrophe if the antennae should fall or collapse. The fire was extinguished and there was no major damage, and the station was soon on the air.

While still in Phoenix I took a U.S. civil service exam, the "JPA" (junior professional assistant). This placed me "on the register" for the Denver area, and I was "within reach" (one of the top three on the register). Also, during this time I was offered a job with the U.S. Forest Service, which would have been with the Kaibab National Forest, north of the Grand

Canyon. Since this was so remote and since I was contemplating marriage, I turned down this offer.

After becoming engaged, I quit my job in Phoenix and moved to Dallas. After some job hunting I took a job as an accountant in the Dallas District Office of the Firestone Tire and Rubber Company. We had about a dozen Firestone stores in a 75-mile radius of Dallas as well as the district office and distribution facilities.

While I was with Firestone I had my "JPA" eligibility transferred to the Dallas Civil Service Office. While it was in limbo, I was approached by the Social Security Regional Office in Dallas and offered a job as field representative trainee in the Santa Fe, New Mexico, district office. I really didn't want this but while I deliberated, they told me the "1950 Amendments to the Social Security Act" were imminent and there would be "lots of other jobs to consider." On the strength of this, I turned down the Santa Fe office. Sure enough, the legislation passed and within a few weeks they offered me a job as claims representative trainee in the Lufkin, Texas, district office. Again, I was not enthusiastic, mainly because I knew Lufkin had a paper mill and I was acquainted with the downwind effects of the paper mill in Bogalusa, Louisiana. Since I was "within reach" on the Dallas register, they accepted my reluctance and next offered me a claims representative trainee job in a new office they were opening in Longview. This one I accepted, and they gave me a choice of entering on duty and starting my training at either the Dallas district office (where I was living) or moving to Tyler and starting there. I chose Tyler since it was close to Longview and half the counties to be served by Longview would be transferred from Tyler.

I entered on duty at the Tyler district office on October 15, 1950, as a GS-5, CRT (Claims Representative Trainee). A few weeks later I went by train to the SSA National Headquarters in Baltimore, Maryland, for three weeks of intensive training. After returning to Tyler, the Longview office still wasn't ready to open yet so I spent about a month in the Tyler district office.

When the space and personnel were finally ready and they opened the Longview district office, I made the move there. We were very busy with the influx of claims for Social Security resulting from the recent legislation. Also, we continued training and studying for a test that would enable us to promote to the "journeyman" position of "claims representative" GS-6. Before I left Longview, I was promoted again to the GS-7 "field representative" position. They then worked out a three-way swap (the only one I ever knew of) in which the FR in San Angelo went to Paris, the CR in Paris went to Longview, and I went to FR in San Angelo.

While I was in San Angelo I traveled a 13-county service area and was an unofficial assistant to the manager. Also, the FR position was re-classified from GS-7 to GS-8. Later when there was a vacancy in the manager position I was the "officer in charge" as acting manager. Also, about this time I was offered a job as claims supervisor, GS-8, in the San Antonio district office, which I declined.

Then I was offered the job of assistant district manager in Austin, GS-10, and I jumped at the chance (skipping the GS-9 level). That proved to be a challenging and interesting job, but not one I wanted to stay in too long. I was delighted when they offered me the job of district manager in Bryan, Texas, and I acquired that title on May 7, 1957. After I was promoted to district manager in Bryan, I received a card of congratulation

HOLLY REES, DISTRICT MANAGER, SOCIAL SECURITY OFFICE
BRYAN, TEXAS MAY 1957

from a former co-worker and on it he wrote: "May you always have enough success to keep you happy and enough failure to keep you humble." I still remember this after 50 years.

Up until this time we had moved a lot and didn't stay in one place very long. We more or less assumed that we would be moving on, but the job was re-classified from a GS-10 to GS-11, to GS-12, to GS-13 and finally to GM-13. I stayed in this position for 27 years until I retired.

During my tenure as DM, my staff ranged from as few as seven people up to 45. This meant a lot of recruiting, training and turnover. Other major activities included speeches for schools and civic clubs, area and regional conferences, and national meetings in Baltimore. If I do say so myself, I ran a good office (with a lot of good people) and received several meritorious step increases and an outstanding office award from the commissioner.

HOLLY REESE PRESENTED WITH THE SOCIAL SECURITY COMMISSION CITATION FOR EXCELLENCE IN MANAGEMENT

When I reached age 55 in 1981 I was eligible to retire, but I really wasn't ready just yet. It was nice to be eligible and to have my "KMA" card, but I thought working longer would not only up my retirement pay but could even develop character. When I decided I had enough character (and enough retirement pay) after about three and a half years, I retired on July 1, 1984. My mother, who had dementia, had come to live with us a year earlier and my mother-in-law died the following January. Between these, new grandchildren and our own health issues, retirement proved to be very well timed.

# 16

## Church, Faith, and Religion

*"I had been a "Christian" and church member for 19 years but was forever changed! I like to say that my religion was all in my head up to that time, that through the lay witness mission it dropped to my heart. Not only was I deeply changed but nearly the entire church was also moved."*

**Because I was not brought up in a Christian** curch as a child, I was not familiar with scripture, prayer and public or private worship. I was superficially exposed to Sunday school, first in the Christian Science Church and then the Congregational Church. Later in the Boy Scouts and school and through weddings, funerals, etc., I saw more of the public image of religion.

I think my parents had had some religious upbringing and leanings, but my dad especially was put off by the hypocrisy of church people saying one thing and doing/living another. A good friend of mine was Catholic, and he could carouse on Saturday night as long as he went to confessions Sunday morning. I, too, observed a lack of sincerity and consistency and was not drawn to this way of life. (I could carouse with him with no qualms!)

A number of my friends were Mormons and even though I didn't understand or accept their beliefs, I had great admiration and respect for their sincere and consistent lives.

Later in the Army, I randomly (i.e., seldom) attended the non-denominational Protestant services. As we moved closer to and participated in combat, the call to be a Christian grew stronger. The person who coined the expression, "There are no atheists in foxholes," and the one who wrote, "Coming in on a wing and a prayer," captured the prevailing feelings. Also, Irving Berlin grasped the country's mood with "God Bless America."

I was not an atheist and not even an agnostic. I was just drifting and indifferent and very much in need of someone to lead me to Christ. This pattern, and a busy life, continued on through college.

When I met and started dating Betty, I soon learned that true happiness and certainly contentment did not come from a bottle, can or keg. As our relationship grew and as I contemplated marriage and a family, I rationalized the necessity of my joining the church and us taking our children to Sunday school and church.

Thus, as an intellectual act, I joined Lakewood Methodist church in Dallas, Texas, on "profession of faith," and began a lifelong affinity to the Methodist church. In succeeding years I served faithfully in a number of positions and became consistent in my giving and attendance. I was always acutely aware of the need to "walk the talk" and not to just "talk the walk." If you had asked me then if I was a Christian, I would have sincerely assured you that I was.

After moving from Dallas we visited several Methodist churches in Tyler and joined the Wesley Methodist Church in Longview. Our son, Lane, was born while we lived in Longview. When we moved to San Angelo, Texas, we visited the First Methodist Church and later were invited to start a new church on the west side. We became charter members of St. Luke's MC. Both of our daughters were born in San Angelo and baptized at St. Luke's. I was asked to teach a Sunday school class and had not given a "yes or no" when we went on vacation to Arizona (July 1952). I worked all day, went home and packed, and we left San Angelo about dusk. We drove all night and at daybreak the next morning right on the continental divide, I fell asleep and totaled the big old Buick I was driving. It was nothing short of a miracle that Betty, Lane and I walked away from the accident. I had a compulsion to phone San Angelo and tell them I'd teach the Sunday school class. I *knew* that I had been spared, again, for something. The nearest phone was over a hundred miles away and by the time we got back to San Angelo I declined the offer to teach.

Next, we moved to Austin and visited several churches before joining Shettles Memorial MC. Betty taught a children's class, and I was assistant teacher for a fifth and sixth grade class. When we moved to Bryan, we visited several churches and fell in love with St. Paul's MC. Again, I threw myself into the activities of the church and eventually filled almost all the jobs they had except choir and music.

In 1969 our beloved pastor, Rev. Guy Pry, encouraged us to have a "lay witness mission." I was on the planning committee and thought that all the meetings and plans were "overkill" (my experience with numerous revivals was that they were okay but seldom had any lasting effect). When the weekend of the LWM finally arrived, we had about 30 men and women from all over East Texas come to St. Paul's to share with us their witness and Christian growth and experiences. It was a fantastic weekend from Friday night through Sunday afternoon when the visitors went home. Sunday night we had an evaluation meeting, and the Holy Spirit was alive and well and leading. That meeting was, without a doubt, the most profound and deeply moving Christian experience in my life. I had been a "Christian" and church member for 19 years but was forever changed! I like to say that my religion was all in my head up to that time, that through the Lay Witness Mission it dropped to my heart. Not only was I deeply changed but nearly the entire church was also moved.

During the years that followed, Bible study, share groups, prayer groups, mission projects, giving and our members going to other churches to participate in their Lay Witness Mission mushroomed. The LWM not only had a dramatic immediate impact on St. Paul's but also had a long lasting and growing effect.

Another area that has been near and dear to my heart and very meaningful is our "Tuesday-Thursday Prayer Group."

It began in the spring of 1972 when Jim Keller was driving back to Bryan from a lay witness mission somewhere. He felt God laying on his heart to start an intercessory prayer group. He presented this calling to our Sunday night praise service, the Holy Spirit led our church to respond, and the rest is history. We decided to meet twice a week and since evenings and weekends are busy, we'd meet Tuesday and Thursday mornings before going to work. We have completed 44 years of this prayer ministry.

The response was enthusiastic and we had some days with over 40 men in attendance. Over time, it settled into a fairly dependable one to15 men and eventually involved a half dozen. We currently have four. For a long time we were referred to as the "Men's Prayer Group." Over the years we have had three or four ladies regularly participate and prefer the "Tuesday-Thursday Prayer Group" designation. We have always welcomed anyone who wanted to come and pray with us, whether as a visitor or permanently. Some people have been very regular and some, who traveled or had other hindrances, came when they could.

We first met in the church office, library or fellowship hall (spilling out on the lawn on nice days). Then the pastor's office and later a Sunday school class room. After we sold the church property and I became more house bound (about seven years ago), we started meeting in my living room, where we still meet. Jim Keller and I are the only ones left from the beginning.

We usually read and discussed some scripture before our "PPI" (praise, petition and intercession) time. We use a fairly lengthy prayer list, by categories. We never lack for prayer requests but have always had a problem with follow-up—not getting feedback on the resolution of the situation for which we were praying. Some requests are temporary or one time only, but most are continuing.

It has been a real blessing and vital element in my Christian life to fellowship at God's throne of grace and bring our petitions to intercede for the needs of others.

I was asked to be church treasurer, which I did for 15 years. I also served as chairman of the administrative board, the council of ministries and the trustees, plus numerous other jobs.

We had an active "United Methodist Men" group and we attended the Conference Men's Retreat at Lakeview Methodist Assembly in the spring and fall for many years. I would estimate about 75 trips to Lakeview, which is near Palestine, Texas. I also participated in other district committee activities. In 2002 Jim Keller and I were recognized as the "Men of the Year" at St. Paul's.

Among the many Bible studies and weekend conferences that we had, one Precept Bible Study was especially meaningful to me. We had been going for several weeks when at home studying I had the most profound and personal revelation that Christ had died for me! Not only "them," "you" and "us" but "me"!

The men of the Rees family attending the Conference Men's Retreat, Lakeview Methodist Assembly near Palestine, Texas

# 17

## AVOCATIONS AND PUBLIC SERVICE

*"Other than Rotary or church, I tried to ration my time to put family first, job second and community activities next."*

## HANDYMAN PROJECTS

BUILDING ON THE EXAMPLE SET BY MY FATHER I have always accumulated and maintained a number of hand and power tools. With these, and the skills he taught me, and a "can do" attitude, I have successfully completed a number of projects, both large and small. Several are memorable.

While living in Dallas I made a shadow box picture frame to house and display my Army medals and insignia. I later made a matching one for Gil's. In Longview I made a plywood cabinet to house Lane's diapers and formula paraphernalia. Later this was used for toys, laundry supplies and is now used to store food staples.

Things boomed and in San Angelo I transformed our backyard with a 15- x 18-foot concrete patio and connecting sidewalks. To that I added a field stone barbecue pit 6-feet long with two 6-feet planters on either side with overhead lights, lawn and pecan trees. We had a veritable oasis. On a more practical side, I installed clothesline poles and clotheslines. The welder had ready-made poles with 18 inches to be set in concrete. I had him make mine with 30 inches to be buried. The caliche was so hard I thought I would never get the holes dug! All of the concrete was mixed by hand in a wheelbarrow. To finish off the backyard project, I made redwood picnic table and bench combinations and a smaller one for the kids.

One final project in San Angelo was to design and build a wall tool cabinet to hold my hand tools and to be able to close the doors and lock the cabinet. The biggest and best addition to my "tool collection" (as my wife referred to it—although she liked the projects I completed) was a Shopsmith, which I still have and use regularly. It will continue to meet my declining needs as

LANE REES CIRCA 1958, SAN ANGELO, TEXAS
REDWOOD TABLE, PLANTER AND BBQ PIT BUILT BY HOLLY

long as I am around, but I can't help but covet the newer, fancier models they are making now.

Later to make a portable barbeque pit, I got a 55-gallon drum (used for shortening) from a bakery and made it vertically with a lazy Susan for the meat and a fire grate that moved up and down with a windlass. It had storage on the bottom below the cutoff drum and shelves on the sides for food and utensils. Someone said it looked like an airplane, but my dad said it would never get off the ground, since it weighed a ton. We used it for some 40-plus years and since it stayed outside, it gradually rusted and deteriorated. I finally gritted my teeth and tossed it (with help) in the dumpster.

When we moved to Bryan and the kids started school, the projects grew in numbers and variety. Later, in college and with families of their own, the pace never let up.

I have made many sandboxes (usually with covers to keep the cats out), dog houses (including one humongous one for two dogs— two rooms!), workbenches, desks, bookcases, lecterns, picture frames, table lamps and other miscellaneous furniture. When Ann left for college, we still had a sedan and I realized that we needed a moving van. I settled on an International Travelall and later a Chevrolet Suburban. Besides all the covered space to haul stuff, I always carried a tool box of essentials for projects away from home. Of course, the big vehicles had to be supplemented with U-Haul trailers and/or trucks when moving days came for the kids.

PORTABLE METAL BBQ PIT BUILT BY HOLLY CIRCA 1954

Other projects were: a coin cabinet, a jewelry cabinet, a media cabinet (made from a Sony TV), clock shelf, a "truck" bed for Brian, and names of the five grandchildren for their bedroom walls. I, also, remodeled our bathroom.

Between college dorms and later homes, I did the following chores for the kids: moving, painting, installing curtain rods, blinds, towel bars, ceiling fans, garage door openers, doggy doors, dryer vents and shelving in closets and garages. When Lane lived in Anchorage, we visited them and I made a playhouse for Brian and Lauren.

The men of our church had a project to re-roof houses for the elderly, widows or needy, which was very worthwhile and satisfying. This mission expanded and came to include installing vinyl siding on older frame houses. To show our versatility, we also installed a number of chain link fences. These were usually weekend projects and besides the handwork and skills, they provided many hours of fellowship.

When my dad died in 1971 I had my pick of his tools. I did take a few things and would have loved to have his metal lathe and welding equipment, etc., but I didn't really need them and didn't have room for them. As I approached retirement, I acquired a few power tools—small band saw, drill press, jig saw, etc. and thought I would be busy with my hobby in retirement.

Probably the largest single project I have undertaken was about ten years ago. The front of our yard (lawn) had a steep shoulder and was very hard and

TOYS HOLLY MADE FOR HIS CHILDREN, EARLY 1950S

6" MULTICOLORED NAME SETS HOLLY MADE FOR EACH GRANDCHILD

dangerous to mow. I considered landscape wood, railroad ties and brick to build a wall, then fill in the gap and level out the yard. I also wanted to widen the concrete driveway and extend the garage forward about 6 1/2 feet. This was a sequential project in three phases.

The retaining wall was Phase 1 and involved digging out for the "castle

HOLLY'S HOME WITH WALL, BRYAN, TEXAS

wall" and building the wall. It was about 90 feet long and four bricks high, with about 240 bricks. Each castle wall brick weighs 28 pounds (dry) and there were about 3 1/2 tons of bricks.

Phase 2 was to dig out the dirt for widening the driveway and use it to backfill the wall and level the yard then to set the forms and prepare the re-enforcing mesh and rebar. I happened to mention this to a dear friend and local builder, Joe Courtney, who said, "You can't do that, you're an old man." (I was about 75 at the time.) He insisted that he send his cement crew to pour and finish the driveway. There was more to it than I anticipated, and his crew of a half dozen experts took several hours and did a great job.

The last time we had the roof replaced, I had them re-frame the house-garage configuration and extend the garage roof forward. Phase 3 was to frame in this enlargement of the garage, cover it with plywood and vinyl siding and get a new overhead door. After completing all this, I built shelving and re-arranged stuff and, finally, was able to keep the car in the garage.

# Rotary International

## Growing up and as a young adult I always felt

that the Rotary Club was the elite of service clubs and hoped to become a member. When we moved to Bryan and I became SSA District Manager in 1956, I was invited to become a Rotarian. I am now completing my 54th year. In 1962 I became club president and during my term we hosted the President of Rotary International, Nitish Laharry of Calcutta, India. This is the only time the Bryan club has ever hosted an RI president.

In 1993 I was honored by Rotary District 5910 by being added to their "Roll of Fame." In 1987, when I had completed 30 years in Rotary, I obtained my first Paul Harris Fellowship. I have since given PHFs to Betty and each of our three children and a second for myself, making six in all.

In August 2007, the Bryan Rotary Club recognized me for 50 years membership and for being the longest continuous member.

August 1, 2007—Bryan, Texas Rotary Club President Prof. Ron Hammond recognizes Holly for 50 years of service (L-R, Prof. Hammond, Holly's daughter Ellen, Holly Rees)

Other than Rotary or church, I tried to ration my time to put family first, job second and community activities next. Some other organizations and activities that I have been involved with include: Boy Scouts, Brazos Church Pantry, Combined Federal Campaign, Brazos County Federal Employees Credit Union, Council of Governments, Council of Civic Clubs, Council of Social Agencies, Crestview Retirement Home, Oak Terrace Neighborhood Association, American Red Cross, schools, veterans organizations.

# IN RECOGNITION

## 2007

## Maintaining Quality of Life Volunteer/Family Caregiver of the Year

Presented to
Holly Rees

In Appreciation for your Outstanding Dedication

# 18

## HEALTH AND CARE GIVING

*"Probably the biggest health event in my life was being shot by a Japanese sniper. I have been able to lead a fairly normal life but have always been acutely aware of what I can and cannot do. The times that I have exceeded my limits have been stressful, and I have learned to pace myself, give up nonessentials, and save my strength for the important things."*

BOTH MY WIFE AND I ENJOYED GOOD HEALTH FOR MOST of our lives, but there have been some things that have had a profound effect on us. I will walk us through our lives in basically chronological order.

Gil and I had our tonsils removed at the same time in our pre-school years. After I finished the first grade, I had acidosis and colitis and stayed out of school for a year of rest and recovery. Rather extreme myopia (nearsightedness) and glasses also shaped my boyhood and life.

Betty had asthma and allergies (which helped bring us together) and had all four wisdom teeth pulled at the same time, which she frequently mentioned, so it was to her a big deal.

Probably the biggest health event in my life was being shot by a Japanese sniper. This "GSW" (gunshot wound) not only resulted in two surgeries and three months in Army hospitals, it also resulted in the Veterans Administration awarding me a permanent 10 percent service-connected disability rating. I have been able to lead a fairly normal life but have always been acutely aware of what I can and cannot do. The times that I have exceeded my limit have been stressful, and I have learned to pace myself, give up non-essentials and save my strength for the important things.

After I was released from the hospital for "limited duty," I tried bowling and dancing and found out that these were too much for me. As a result, I never danced with my loving wife of 63 years.

About six months after we married, Betty became pregnant with our first child. The second one was born a couple of years later, and our third child arrived 14 months afterwards. All three of our children were born within a little over four years after we were married. We used to kid that with 27 months of pregnancy, over half our married life had been in that state. We were always glad our children were close together and have remained close to this day.

When I turned 55, I was diagnosed with Type 2, non-insulin-dependent diabetes. We decided to try and control it with diet and exercise. We have been rather strict and consistent with the diet for 35 years now. Since I had been shot in the foot, I couldn't jog, and walking was tenuous. I decided the bicycle was the best exercise for me. As a result, I try to ride at least six days a week and usually ride 12 miles a day. I have averaged over 2,000 miles a year and have logged over 60,000 miles. I am on my sixth bicycle.

Once a neighbor asked if I thought having diabetes had been a blessing. An inconvenience, yes, a problem, maybe, but a blessing? Then she said I probably wouldn't be riding my bike and watching my diet and being so healthy otherwise . . . so it really has been a blessing.

When we turned 65, Betty said, "Now that we're 65, we're falling apart," to which I replied, "Where do you get this *we* stuff?" I spoke rashly, and we both ended up with some health issues.

It seems insignificant, but I had a problem with hiccups. They came on during lunch or supper (never breakfast) and would last for some time. My doctor suggested things but they never worked, and I never felt he took this seriously enough. Finally after many years he sent me to a gastroenterologist, who did an "EGD" (esophagogastroduodenscopy), and I went for many years without a hiccup, with only an occasional bout to this day.

Betty had severe bunions and at age 64 was diagnosed with low-tension glaucoma. The glaucoma was "front burner" and on January 2, 1991, she had a bi-lateral trabeculectomy at Presbyterian Hospital in Dallas. There were complications, and she never drove the car again and later was declared "legally blind." Later that year she had bilateral bunionectomy surgery at Baylor Hospital in Dallas.

Along the way, I had hernia surgery, cataracts removed from both eyes (which enabled me to scrap the one-half inch-thick glasses and wear normal ones) and a contra costal separation (from a bicycle accident). Seven years ago I started having severe abdominal pain, and CT scans revealed diverticulitis with severe infection. After antibiotics failed to solve the problem, I had surgery to remove 10 inches of my colon and my appendix. It was at this time I could no longer be the sole, full-time care provider for Betty and started my relationship with Home Instead Senior Care.

Betty had been obsessive-compulsive for some time, but we just lived with it. I think this blinded us to the beginning phases of Alzheimer's. Finally her internist regular doctor referred her to a neurologist. After an electroencephalogram and a CT scan, he said she had suffered some ministrokes and pronounced a diagnosis of multi-infarct dementia. July 2011 was the thirteenth anniversary of this diagnosis, although we know now that it was coming on for several years before that.

We both have had a mild problem with skin cancer and have had some pre-cancerous lesions frozen and a few surgically removed. Prior to the cataract surgeries, a retinologist from Austin said I needed a "scleral sling" to slow/stop my malignant (i.e., progressive) myopia. It sounded gruesome, risky and not appealing to me and since many other specialists recommended against doing it, I never did.

Two further items to mention: five years ago on a Saturday morning I passed out and very reluctantly allowed someone to take me to the emergency room. I was admitted and for four days they ran every cardiovascular test they had (EKG, stress test, echo cardiogram, catheterization, ultrasound, etc.) and could find no CV problem. The final diagnosis was vasovagal syncope, and that has been the only time that has happened.

Last summer Betty developed a rash on her stomach that spread around to her back and got infected. When we became aware of this, we took her to the doctor and found it was the shingles.

Everyone I have ever known with shingles said it was very painful and the itching was terrible. This may be a by-product of the haze of Alzheimer's, but Betty did not appear to be in pain or scratch excessively.

During my junior and senior high school years, Grandmother Rees, who had one leg amputated as a result of diabetes, came to live with us. My dear mother was her caregiver for years and set an example of "TLC" (tender loving care). Since there were no girls in the family, I often got involved in helping Mom with her care.

Fast forward a few years and Mom is given a pacemaker and diagnosed with multi-infarct dementia and probably Alzheimer's. We brought her here, and Betty became her caregiver, again setting an example for TLC for over seven years she lived with us. We finally and reluctantly had to put her in a nursing home, and seven months later she died of a stroke.

Sociological studies have shown that when a spouse or close relative gets sick, the wives rise to the occasion and become caregivers. But often when it's the wife who gets sick, the husband splits, turns alcoholic or puts her in a nursing home.

I clearly remember our wedding vows, including "for richer or poorer" and especially "in sickness and in health," so when Betty developed Alzheimer's I pledged to do the very best I could to care for her at home and only considered a nursing home as a last resort. Two books that have made an impression on me are Burkett's *Last Light* and McQuilkens' *A Promise Kept*. Both books are by ministers who gave up their work to care for their wives with Alzheimer's. Both of these accounts very closely parallel my own experience.

As the Alzheimer's gradually and inexorably progressed, it became more and more apparent that I needed help and could no longer be the sole caregiver. At first I hired a Blinn College nursing student for a few hours a week. Later I went with Home Instead Senior Care, scheduling a caregiver to take over for me every morning of the week for three hours, plus an extra hour on Sunda, and six hours on Wednesday. During that morning time I would grocery shop, ride my bike, and run other errands. On special occasions (graduations, weddings, a trip to the World War II Museum in New Orleans, etc.), I arranged 24-hour care for Betty. I eventually added a three-hour evening shift to the schedule.

Several years ago the Alzheimer's Support Group nominated me for Caregiver of the Year Award for a seven-county region. I was a little miffed when they gave it to a person who was clearly a "volunteer" and not a "caregiver," and so I forgot about this award.

In April 2007 just before my trip to the Far East, I was honored with Caregiver of the Year-Family Award. It seems that our Home Instead lady, Georgetta Wilson, had nominated me for the honor. Coincidentally I had nominated her for Caregiver of the Year-Professional (paid) category, and she was picked to be so honored. I was not so impressed with the ego boost or honor as I was pleased with the verification that we must have been doing something right.

This confirmed my desire to provide the best possible care for Betty as long as I could. She took care of me and our family, and my mother, for nearly 50 years. I counted it a blessing, a pleasure and an obligation to care for her "'til death us do part." I prayed that I would outlive Betty so that I could be around to care for her. I also prayed for strength, guidance and the good health I needed in order to care for her.

As I neared the end of writing this book, I purchased two burial spaces for Betty and myself in the new "Memorial Cemetery of College Station." The cemetery was originally advertised and promoted for the "Aggie Field of Honor" section for alumni and other persons connected with Texas A&M University, but it also includes sections for the general public.

In April 2013, Betty suffered a stroke that sent her first to St. Joseph Hospital in Bryan, and then to the Hospice Brazos Valley in-patient facility. She died on April 24th, 2013, one day after our sixty-third wedding anniversary. Friends and family attended services for her at the Calloway-Jones Funeral Home. She was buried in the Memorial Cemetary plot I mentioned (see photo above).

# Part Four

## Conflicts & Resolutions

# 19

## Return to Okinawa

*"We had lunch just east of Mabuni and from the map I could tell we were within 300 yards of the place where I was shot by a sniper on June 21, 1945. The sniper was in a cave on the south side of the hill we were on, and I was on the plain below in the village of Udo. It was a moving experience to relive this big event in my life even after 62 years."*

I USED TO ENVY THE PEOPLE WHO HAD SERVED IN THE ETO (European Theater of Operations) and the opportunities that they had to revisit the battlegrounds, cemeteries and other special locations where they had served. This was pretty much true for North Africa, Italy, England, France and other places. I have never heard of anyone or any group that had revisited any of the Pacific Islands, except for some Marines at Iwo Jima and at Pearl Harbor.

When I got the flyer from the National World War II Museum in New Orleans telling about their planned trip to Okinawa and the Far East in 2007, I got excited.

The first step was to contact my two daughters and see if they could come to stay with and care for Betty. They worked it out for Ann to come first, then Ellen would come and they would both be here together for several days. Later Ann returned home and Ellen would stay until we returned. I arranged for the Home Instead ladies to keep coming every morning so Ann and Ellen wouldn't have to be here 24/7.

With that major hurdle out of the way, I then invited my son Lane to be my guest on the trip. I told him I would pay for everything except souvenirs and alcohol and asked him to be our photographer. He had a meeting to get rearranged but jumped at the chance.

The next step was to plan a visit to the Museum in New Orleans. I had correspondence and phone calls with Stephen and Karen there and wanted Lane and me to visit the Museum before our trip. My daughter Ellen came here from Alexandria, Louisiana, and drove me back to their home. The next day Ellen and Ron drove me to New Orleans. Lane and Brenda drove over from Florida, and we met at the Museum and enjoyed a tour of the very impressive array of World War II memorabilia. We enjoyed New Orleans cuisine, spent the night and the next day returned to Alexandria, and Ellen brought me home the next day. This was in July 2006.

The following months involved getting a passport, shots, luggage, clothing and arranging for the money needed for the trip. Then, getting plane reservations and tickets, trip and health and accident insurance and any other loose ends tied down.

Lane was the chairman of the Board of Trustees for the Methodist Foundation for Evangelism. He went to his rescheduled meeting at the Saint Paul School of Theology in Kansas City on April 11-13 then returned to Florida to pack and drive to Bryan, Texas. Ann got here on April 14, and Lane arrived the next day and we were ready to go!

Shortly before we left on Monday, April 16, Georgetta Wilson, the angel from Home Instead who cared for Betty each morning Monday through Friday, came and gave us a digital camera and memory card to use to record our trip. (We ended up with over 800 pictures!)

Our odyssey began when the ground shuttle, a 10-passenger van, picked us up at my house about 2 p.m. on Monday, April 16. There was already an international flavor in the air as everyone on the shuttle was bound for a foreign destination. One young lady was bound for London, a couple for Colombia, a man for Mexico, another person for Taiwan and Lane and I headed for Hong Kong and the driver was from Nicaragua. The shuttle dropped us off at the Marriott Hotel at Bush International Airport in Houston. We had a leisurely supper, got the new digital camera charged and ready and went to bed early. We even went to the airport to make sure how long the drive would take, so as to not be late! After 10 months of preparation and eager anticipation, the time finally arrived.

Early the next morning (like 4 a.m.) we got up and took the shuttle train to the terminal for United Air Lines domestic flights. After checking in and getting rid of our checked luggage, we found a McDonald's and had breakfast. Our flight left at 7 a.m. (which is why we spent the night) and we flew to O'Hare in Chicago. After going to the United non-domestic terminal and as we were waiting for our flight, a young man approached us and asked if we were the Reeses. He was Martin K. A. Morgan (Marty) from the Museum and a resource historian on the trip. It turned out we were the only father/son combination on the trip so were easy to spot. We had a brief, friendly visit before we boarded.

We had tourist accommodations and the leg room was nil, the reclining minimal and the long trip exhausting. Out of O'Hare, we flew pretty much north, maybe a little west, over Canada, the Arctic Circle, very near the North Pole, over the Bering Sea, Siberia, Mongolia, communist China and landed in Hong Kong. After deplaning and getting our luggage, we got in a humongous line for customs. A petite Chinese lady in uniform came up to me and asked if I was over 70. "Way over 70—I'm 81," and she led us from the long line to another station where only one couple was ahead of us. One of the few advantages of old age!

We then met a representative of the Clipper Cruise Line (a subsidiary of Intrav) and boarded a charter bus to the Intercontinental Hotel. We had reservations and quickly checked in and went to our room. Lane wanted to scope things out but I crashed. From the time I got up in Houston until I crashed in Hong Kong was 29 hours with practically no sleep. Between jet leg, sleep deprivation and ankle edema, I was not too well off to start our odyssey. But I quickly recovered.

HOLLY AT THE HONG KONG MUSEUM OF HISTORY

The next morning, greatly refreshed, we had a good breakfast and received a roster for the cruise and a schedule of the planned activities. We were on our own that first day until a group meeting and dinner at the hotel that evening. Lane and I walked (we should have taken a taxi) to the Hong Kong Museum of History, which had an excellent collection of items showing the history of Hong Kong. We had lunch there at the museum and then returned to the hotel.

Because the National World War II Museum was sponsoring the trip and touted Okinawa as the prime spot, I had assumed that we would all be Okinawa veterans and families. I was surprised to learn that there were only four of us who had fought at/on Okinawa: two Marines, one Navy on an offshore destroyer and one Army infantryman—me.

There were several people on the roster that I especially wanted to meet, but Lane and I also planned to mix and try to meet everyone. The first were the Clarks from Modesto, California (where I had spent two months at Hammond General Hospital). Lowell was the Navy vet from the destroyer USS *Wren* and was accompanied by his wife Pat, son Randy and daughter-in-law Sandy. Besides being Okinawa veterans and the Modesto connection, Randy and Sandy had two daughters who went to the University of Arizona and Randy had been in the California National Guard 184th Infantry Regiment.

HONG KONG: THE CLARKS FROM MODESTO, CA. (L-R) LOWELL CLARK, NAVY VET WHO SERVED ON THE DESTROYER USS WREN AT OKINAWA, HIS WIFE PAT, SON RANDY, DAUGHTER-IN-LAW SANDY

The next ones I wanted to meet were Mark and Peggy Holly from St. Louis. My mother was born in Fulton, Missouri, and lived near Moberly before moving to Arizona. We all tried to figure out some connection, but never could. Still another group was Dan and Noreen Collins from New Jersey. We were the only father/son group and they were the only father/daughter. My wife's mother was a Collins in Mississippi and I wondered if they could be kin. The Hollys really tried to connect, but I don't think the Collinses were as anxious, especially when they found out we were Republicans and they were staunch Democrats.

I had already read Eugene Sledge's book about "K-3-5-1" (K Company, 3rd Battalion, 5th Marine Regiment, 1st Marine Division) on Peleliu and Okinawa and was delighted to learn that the two Marines were from Sledge's company. R. V. Burgin was a mortar man like Sledge, and Harry Bender was a BAR man. We hit it off from the start and spent a lot of time together. R. V. lives in Lancaster, Texas, and Lane and I have visited him at his home twice now since the trip. Harry lives in Honolulu, and I have heard from him once. They are both written about in Sloan's new book, *The Ultimate Battle*.

HONG KONG: THE TWO US MARINE VETS FROM OKINAWA (L-R) HARRY BENDER, R.V. BURGIN

Lane and I wanted to get a "type set" of each circulating Hong Kong coin for our collections and did the same later for Republic of China (Taiwan) and Japan.

The evening meeting was for orientation and a preview of the coming events. Dr. Don Miller, who wrote *D Days in the Pacific* and was a resource historian on the trip, gave a lecture on the big picture of the situation leading up to the Okinawa campaign, its highlights and accomplishments. At 8 p.m. there was a laser light show all over Hong Kong. Colored lights flashed from the tops of most of the buildings while loudspeakers played music and the lights were coordinated with the music—very impressive! They do this every evening. We spent two nights at the Intercontinental Hotel, which is a 5-star hotel and had a spectacular view of Hong Kong, day and night.

The next morning two large tour buses picked us up and started our tour of Hong Kong. They took us to the base of Victoria Peak and we rode the funicular (I had to look that one up—I was familiar with the aerial trams at El Paso and Albuquerque, but this was more like the cable cars in San Francisco) tram to the top. I had carried my binoculars along, but unfortunately it was foggy and what promised to be a fabulous view was disappointing.

The second stop was the Man Mo temple, which was crowded into busy downtown Hong Kong. It was the first of many shrines and temples that we would visit. The incense smoke was so thick inside that you could hardly see or breathe—I couldn't get out soon enough.

Next it was the Aberdeen area of Hong Kong harbor at Kowloon. We transferred from the buses to sampans and saw the sights at "ground" (er, that is, water) level. We passed sampans where people lived on the water. It was said that people were born, raised, married and died in these sampans. This would have to be very limiting, confining and not my cup of tea.

Hong Kong: harbor view

The Stanley Market (shopping area) was next and was neat, clean, colorful and interesting. They had many shops with a wide variety of items for sale in Hong Kong dollars. We bought some souvenirs for ourselves and for gifts. The main thing I bought was a wall hanging (later framed) from First Corinthians 13:13 with "Faith, Hope and Love" in Chinese Kanji.

By then it was time to eat and we went to a very nice place for "dim sum." Lane had eaten it before and said it was good (Chinese dumplings), but I was disappointed. Then it was back to the Intercontinental Hotel to check out and go, again by bus, to the wharf where we would board our 129-passenger cruise ship, the *Clipper Odyssey*.

HONG KONG: LANE AND HOLLY ABOARD THE **CLIPPER ODDYSSEY**

Each morning we received an itinerary for the day's activities and the nightly programs. Also, "News Clips" to keep us up to date on significant world happenings while we were cut off from television, cell phone, Internet, etc. (A welcome blessing!)

We had a "mandatory security and safety muster drill," wearing our life preservers and getting cued in on our lifeboat assignments. Later we had orientation information by cruise director Noreen Haukland, expedition leader Jane Wilson and hotel director Craig Murray as well as introduction to ship Capt. Frank Allica, the crew and staff. We were also welcomed aboard by Capt. Allica and by National Museum president and CEO Nick Mueller.

The next day, Saturday, April 21, was a full day at sea, going up the coast of Communist China, through the Taiwan straits and heading for Taiwan. During the day we had three lectures in the morning, early afternoon and late afternoon: (1) the Pacific War, 1941-1943, by Hugh Ambrose; (2) the

Pacific War, 1943-1945 by Don Miller; and (3) Taiwan, separate entity or a Chinese province, by Lea Williams.

The evening ended with the captain's cocktail party and dinner, which was a semiformal time.

Taiwan: The Pao-An Temple

Taiwan: The Chiang Lai Schek Memorial

Sunday, April 22, found us docking in Keelung, Taiwan, where we took two buses for the 25- to 30-mile ride south to Taipei. There we visited the National Palace Museum, the Pao-An Temple and the changing of the guard at the Martyrs' Shrine. It reminded me of the changing of the guard at Arlington National Cemetery, with an oriental twist. We feasted on a Mongolian "barbeque," which was a combination of a buffet and a huge communal stir-fry. After lunch we went to the Chiang Kai Shek Memorial Hall, the Chinese Handicraft Center and drove by the "101 Commerce Building," which they said was the world's tallest building (it has since been surpassed). After returning to Keelung and the ship we departed. The evening's lecture was "The U.S. Navy's War and the Battle of Midway" by Hugh Ambrose.

ZODIAC TRIP TO IRIOMOTE ISLAND

On Monday, April 23, we had a morning lecture by our resident ornithologist Brent Stephenson on "Introduction to the Birds of Japan." Later we made our first, of many, Zodiac excursions to Iriomote Island. We took buses (I was amazed that almost everywhere we went there were tour buses waiting to take us to our destinations) from our landing spot to a river where we rode upstream by mangrove trees and colorful subtropical terrain to a landing place. Four of us stayed there while the rest hiked on up higher to Mariudo Falls. They say it was spectacular, but I wanted to save my feet for Okinawa. I had taken a folding cane on the trip and by now I was starting to use it. Back on the *Odyssey* we had another lecture, "Overview of the Battle of Okinawa," by Marty Morgan. That evening we watched the movie, "Price for Peace." Lane had told someone and they gave a champagne toast to me since this was our 57th wedding anniversary.

OKINAWA: HOLLY REES LANDING AT NAHA

OKINAWA: (L-R) MARINE HARRY BENDER, HISTORIAN AND GUIDE HUGH AMBROSE, MARINE R.V. BURGIN, HOLLY REES

At last, the main part of the trip (and the reason I wanted to take the trip) started as we docked in Naha, Okinawa. We were ceremonially welcomed dockside and boarded our buses.

Our first stop was Hagushi (Orange) Beach, where two divisions of Army (7th and 96th) and two divisions of Marines (1st and 5th) had made the initial landing on Okinawa on Easter Sunday, April 1, 1945. We were joined by ex-Marine Chris Majewski, to be our Okinawa guide and resident military authority. He was a walking encyclopedia of facts and figures but was not a participant in the battle.

We were told all morning that we were to have a "box lunch" for lunch. We then went to an elegant, upscale restaurant and had sushi and other delicacies in lacquered "boxes" (hence the name "box lunch"—I had thought Styrofoam boxes and sandwiches but was pleasantly surprised).

OKINAWA: THE ELEGANT "BOX LUNCH"

After lunch we visited Sugarloaf Hill and Shuri Castle. Shuri had been destroyed in the fighting but had been restored.

The evening of Thursday, April 24, they had a panel of the four veterans of Okinawa, moderated by Don Miller. I wore my khaki uniform that I had been discharged in on June 29, 1946, and was joined by Marines R. V. Burgin and Harry Bender, and Navy veteran Lowell Clark. Don guided the discussion, and each of us told about our combat experiences on Okinawa. You could have heard a pin drop, and the audience was glued to our every

OKINAWA: MARINES HARRY BENDER AND R.V. BURGIN AT SHURI CASTLE

OKINAWA: PANEL DISCUSSION OF THEIR COMBAT EXPERIENCES DURING THE US CAMPAIGN TO TAKE OKINAWA. (L-R) US MARINE VETERANS R.V. BURGIN AND HARRY BENDER, MODERATOR DON MILLER, US ARMY VETERAN HOLLY REES, US NAVY VETERAN LOWELL CLARK

word. It was moving for me and I am sure for everyone. I included pictures of my Japanese flag and told about the translation and the shadow box with my medals.

Wednesday, April 25, we went to the Japanese Naval Underground Headquarters. There we met Megan Weatherly (from Nacogdoches, Texas) and Lloyd Wainscott, both from the Okinawa Living magazine. They took

Okinawa: After the panel discussion, Holly tells his story with a display of his sevice awards and the Rising Sun flag (Hinomaru Yosegoui) he took in combat.

Okinawa: The Himeyuri Peace Memorial—Okinawa Prefectural Peace Memorial and Museum, where the eight US veterans in the group lay a wreath on the memorial

pictures and interviewed Lane and me and ran an article in the June 2007 edition, which they sent us. From there we visited the Buckner Memorial where Gen. Simon Bolivar Buckner was killed.

Then we visited the Himeyuri Peace Memorial (Cave of the Virgins), the Okinawa Prefectural Peace Memorial and Museum. The eight World War II veterans placed a floral wreath on the memorial. On the spacious grounds they had many black marble slabs (similar to the Vietnam Wall in Washington, D.C., but made up of many smaller slabs) on which were etched the names of all the Americans, Japanese, and Okinawans killed in the Battle for Okinawa. There were 12,000 Americans, 110,000 Japanese and some 120,000 Okinawans, for a total of about 240,000 dead.

We had lunch just east of Mabuni and from the map I could tell we were within 300 yards of the place where I was shot by a sniper on June 21, 1945. The sniper was in a cave on the south side of the hill we were on, and I was on the plain below in the village of Udo.

OKINAWA: OUTSIDE MABUNI, ABOVE UDO VILLAGE, HOLLY REES STANDS NEAR THE CAVE FROM WHICH THE JAPANESE SNIPER FIRED THE SHOT THAT WOUNDED HIM, 62 YEARS BEFORE.

It was a moving experience to relive this big event in my life even after 62 years. Nothing looked the same as it did then, though. The vegetation was thick, green and lush, and modern concrete block buildings were everywhere.

That evening we had a second panel of veterans (who had served elsewhere from Okinawa). It was also moderated by Don Miller and was very interesting. The participants were John Zettler ("the Commander"), a Seabee; Glen Jostad, Air Corps (who had been shot down and spent nine months in a German prisoner of war camp); Paul Hilliard, Air Corps; and Jack Schultz, a combat infantry veteran who had served in Europe.

Thursday, April 26, we had a leisurely morning to shop in Naha (where I saw a Rotary emblem in a small park), then sailed to Ie Shima island where we took the Zodiacs to shore. The buses took us to the Ernie Pyle memorial (on the site where he was killed) and where we participated in another wreath laying. Then we went on to the Pinnacle, which the young and hearty climbed. Those few of us who were neither young nor hearty stayed at the visitor center at the base of the Pinnacle.

That evening our lecture was by Marty Morgan on "The Kamikaze Pilots," getting us primed for Saturday's tour.

IE SHIIMA: HOLLY AT THE ERNIE PYLE MEMORIAL

Friday, April 27, we had three lectures in the morning, afternoon and evening. The first was "Japan in the Pacific Ring of Fire" by Lea Williams; the second, "Operations Olympic and Coronet" by Marty Morgan; and third, "The Future of the National World War II Museum" by Nick Mueller. We also had a surprise, unscheduled Zodiac landing on Naka No Shima, which is a small, remote volcanic island off the beaten path (no buses!) and more authentic than the other touristy places. It was a treat to get to see this secluded island, which was the last of our island visits, and we were now ready for mainland Japan.

Saturday, April 28, we docked in Kagoshima and rode the buses to Chiran, which was a former Imperial Japanese air base. There we visited a memorial to the kamikaze pilots, a museum, and an ancient samurai village.

CHIRAN: FORMER IMPERIAL JAPANESE AIR BASE
MEMORIAL TO KAMIKAZE PILOTS

SAKURAJIMA ISLAND: LIVE VOLCANO,
ARIMURA OBSERVATORY

Back in Kagoshima, we took a ferry to Sakurajima Island and saw a live volcano and the Arimura lava observatory. A tour of Kagoshima included visiting the Iso gardens. Later that afternoon we had a large contingent of Japanese children board the ship to sing and dance for us. They were all very colorfully dressed and very cute and colorful.

That evening the lecture was by Don Miller on "The Air War."

KAGOSHIMA: JAPANESE CHILDREN
PERFORM ABOARD SHIP

HOLLY AT NAGASAKI HARBOR

We were welcomed into Nagasaki harbor with a fire boat water display on Sunday, April 29. After disembarking we rode the buses to the Peace Memorial Park, the site of the second atomic bomb dropping. I learned two things I didn't know:

NAGASAKI: PEACE MEMORIAL PARK

1. The bombing of Nagasaki was the third choice. The first and second were fogged in, and since they couldn't take the bomb back and didn't want to waste it, they picked Nagasaki.

2. I had assumed that the bomb exploded on impact and wondered why there wasn't a huge crater. The answer was that with a proximity fuse, the bomb exploded about 300 feet in the air.

LANE WITH RUSSIAN NAVY CADETS

We toured the National Atomic Bomb Museum, the "Ground Zero" monument and met a large group of Russian naval cadets. We also toured the Glover Gardens, Ouna Catholic Church and a shopping arcade. Back on the *Odyssey* we were treated to an operatic rendition from Puccini's "Madame Butterfly" (the setting for

HOLLY AND LANE VISIT WITH "MADAME BUTTERFLY" PERFORMERS

which is Nagasaki). There were two female opera singers and a pianist. That evening Don Miller gave a lecture on "Nagasaki, Hiroshima and the Bomb."

We docked at Shimonoseki the next day on Monday, April 30, and rode the buses over a large, modern bridge to Kitakyushu. The first attractions were Kokura Castle and the Mount Hinoyama observatory. An unexpected and unheralded treat was to see a projectile from the Japanese super battleship, the *Yamato*. Our biggest guns on U.S. battleships were 16-inch and the *Yamato* had 18-inch guns. The projectile was huge and an awesome sight, but was a "dud."

KITAKYUSHU: KOKURA CASTLE

MOUNT HINOYAMA OBVSERVATORY

When we returned to the ship we were greeted by a couple of samurai warrior reenactors for a photo op. That afternoon Hugh Ambrose lectured on "The Legacy of World War II." We began our cruise of the "Inland Sea," and the next morning we moored in Hiroshima harbor.

That evening we had a choice of two movies: "An Inconvenient Truth" or "Japanland: The Final Test."

On Tuesday, May 1, we made our only "wet" landing in the Zodiacs on Miyajima Island. This was only the second time that we didn't have tour buses to transport us (Naka No Island) but didn't have too far to walk.

HOLLY AND LANE POSE WITH SAMURAI WARRIOR REENACTORS

MIYAJIMA ISLAND: HOLLY AND LANE AT SHINTO MONASTERY

There was a large and colorful Shinto shrine, monastery and pagoda. Also, "the most photographed place in Japan," the Torii out in the water in front of the shrine. We also saw lots of tame deer, a rickshaw and another shopping area. We returned to the ship and went on to dock in Hiroshima.

After still another bus ride we visited the site of the first atomic bomb detonation. They had a peace park and museum there as well as the Atomic Bomb Dome, a reinforced concrete building that had survived the bomb blast and was left as a memorial. There was also a large mound that was a communal grave for thousands of unidentified bodies.

HIROSHIMA: HOLLY VISITS THE DOME IN HIROSHIMA, SITE OF THE HIROSHIMA PEACE PARK AND MUSEUM, GROUND ZERO FOR THE DETONATION OF THE FIRST ATOMIC BOMB ("LITTLE BOY") USED IN WAR AUGUST 6, 1945

HIROSHIMA: THE COMMUNAL GRAVE, WITH SHINTO AND BUDDHIST MARKERS, FOR ALL THE UNIDENTIFED DEAD AFTER THE HIROSHIMA BOMBING

That evening they had the captain's farewell cocktail party and dinner, and showed a DVD "slide show" of pictures taken by the cruise staff on the trip. We later were given the DVD to take home with us to help keep alive the memories. We took about 800 pictures ourselves and with the DVD have a treasure trove of pictures.

On Wednesday, May 2, we docked and disembarked at Kobe, marking the end of the cruise. Those not staying for the post-cruise extension were bused to either of the Osaka airports.

PORT OF KOBE            HOLLY AT TODA-JI TEMPLE

We, being reduced in number, rode in a single bus through Osaka and on to Nara. There we visited the Todai-ji temple and the Yasuga shrine, saw more tame deer and had lunch at the Nara Hotel, a small authentic

Japanese hotel. The bus drove us on to Kyoto and our next accommodation at the 5-star Hotel Okura. It was nice and colorful, but the view was nothing to compare with the Intercontinental Hotel in Hong Kong. That evening Lane and I teamed up with Dan and Noreen Collins for an interesting and authentic Japanese meal. We couldn't decide what to order (or what some of the choices were!), so we finally ordered four different items and extra plates so we could pick and choose family style.

Before our trip I had borrowed a Rotary International directory and made a list of all the Rotary Clubs in all the places we would visit. There were several hundred in all, including four in Naha, 16 on Okinawa and many in all the major cities. Some met in the morning, some at noon and some in the evening. Every day of the week was used and many meeting places, mostly hotels. I wanted to "make up," i.e., visit, at least one Rotary Club in the Orient. After studying the long list of clubs and comparing the list to our scheduled itinerary, it looked like the one we could visit (me as a Rotarian and Lane as my guest) met on the morning of Thursday, May 3, at the Hotel Okura. After supper Lane and I scoped out the meeting room where they were to meet the following morning. Guess what? Thursday, May 3, was a national holiday and the Rotary Club did not meet! Therefore, we did not get to visit a Rotary Club. We did see the Rotary emblem in a number of hotels, parks and public places, which confirmed the active presence of Rotary in the Far East.

After a nice breakfast buffet in the Orizonte lounge on the top of the Hotel Okura, we began our tour of Kyoto. The Golden Pavilion and the luxurious wisteria flowers had to be the prettiest single sight on the entire trip. Then we visited the Ryonanji Rock Garden and yet another shrine, the Heian Shinto Shrine. By this time we had seen so many temples (Buddhist) and shrines (Shinto) on the trip that they had lost their novelty.

Lane was on the Texas A&M University International Board (his

KYOTO: THE GOLDEN PAVILION

KYOTO: HOLLY AND LANE MEET WITH FRIENDS ROGELIO AND NATSU AT THE HOTEL OKURA

alma mater), which began when he worked for ARCO International and was traveling to many foreign locations, including an oilfield in Algeria. At one of the committee meetings he had met a young lady from Nagoya, Japan. When he found out that we would be visiting Kyoto, he e-mailed her and we tried to arrange a meeting. After our morning tour, we met Natsu and her boyfriend, Rogelio, in the colorful lobby of the Hotel Okura.

To add to the story, Rogelio was from Taxco, Mexico, had earned his Ph.D. in engineering at Texas A&M (where they met) and was currently working and living in Mexico City. He was visiting Natsu in Nagoya and they had taken the "bullet train" to Kyoto to meet us. The rest of the *Odyssey* tour group had gone to a geisha house and theater for the afternoon. We decided to go to the Universal Studios, where most of the Japanese television programs and movies are filmed.

We saw the sets and many actors and actresses there and even a live ninja theater program. It was very interesting and informative—and apparently better than the geisha afternoon the others had.

When we returned to the Hotel Okura it was time for supper and the four of us ate at the Orrizonte lounge. It was nice enough, but not wonderful and when I picked up the tab it was the most expensive meal I had ever had. Later I said I had never eaten octopus and Lane said, "Yes, you have," along with sushi and who knows what else.

HOLLY AND LANE POSE WITH ACTORS AT UNIVERSAL STUDIOS, KYOTO

The next morning, Friday, May 4, Lane and I went for a walk in downtown Kyoto. Amid all the Japanese signs and businesses we stumbled upon a place called "Holly's Café!" Lane got a cup of coffee, and we got some matches and napkins as souvenirs and took a picture of me at the front.

HOLLY FINDS "HOLLY'S CAFE" IN DOWNTOWN KYOTO, JAPAN

This reminded me of the first time I visited Fredericksburg, Texas. Driving down the main street past the Nimitz Hotel (Fredericksburg is the hometown of Fleet Adm. Chester Nimitz, and the hotel is now the National World War II Pacific Theater Museum), every business is German—Schultz, Krause, etc.—and suddenly you see O'Brian's Café.

We later rode a chartered bus to the Kansai International Airport in Osaka. In Nagasaki Lane and I each bought a colorful and attractive ceramic decanter filled with sochu (a liquor made from sweet potatoes). I had mine in my checked luggage, and Lane had his in his carry-on. In customs and security they told Lane he couldn't take it on board with him, so he reluctantly watched as they were going to throw it away in a trash barrel. Just before the fateful pitch, Lane asked if they could just empty the sochu and give him the decanter. He said to me, "Since you're not interested in the sochu, will you trade with me when we get to Bryan?" Which is what we did.

We boarded United Air Lines Flight 886 for the long trip to San Francisco, which I was dreading (remembering the flight from Chicago to Hong Kong). We had just settled in our economy class seats when a flight attendant came up and said the captain had invited us to be his guests in the business class section. We almost broke our necks rushing to accept his offer.

The business class seats were wider, softer and reclined much more, with adequate leg room. The food and drinks were also much better. In case you are wondering, Lane has a friend in Florida who flies for United but who was off on sick leave. Leslie Prothrow and her family are members of the church Lane attends. She had e-mailed the crew that we would be on that flight and to "take good care of us," which they did. One of the flight attendants even asked if we were brothers!

After an actually enjoyable flight we landed in San Francisco IAP, went through customs and boarded United Flight 378 for Houston. They said there would be a delay as they were checking out a problem with the brakes. After over an hour on the plane they transferred us to another plane and we left about two hours behind schedule. So, when we arrived at Houston IAP, we had missed our ground shuttle connection and we had to take a later one, finally arriving home in Bryan about 10:30 p.m.

Before making the trip I had felt sure that it would be moving to return to Okinawa, colorful and interesting to see the Far East and a good chance to spend "quality time" with Lane. It turned out to be even better than I had anticipated, but I wondered how it had affected Lane.

Recently I received a copy of *UMMEN*, the magazine of the United Methodist men, Winter 2008 edition. In the centerfold was an article that Lane had written about our trip and reading it removed any doubts about how the trip had impacted him. His life was "enriched," and the contact with the World War II veterans "helped me to appreciate the sacrifices made…." "It was touching to hear my father share his memories…." He reminisced about the life-changing lay witness mission we shared in 1969. "I am glad my father invited me to see where he served in the Second World War." "We have wonderful memories to share together in the years ahead."

As mentioned in the Foreword, Lane has been a big motivation for me to write this book.

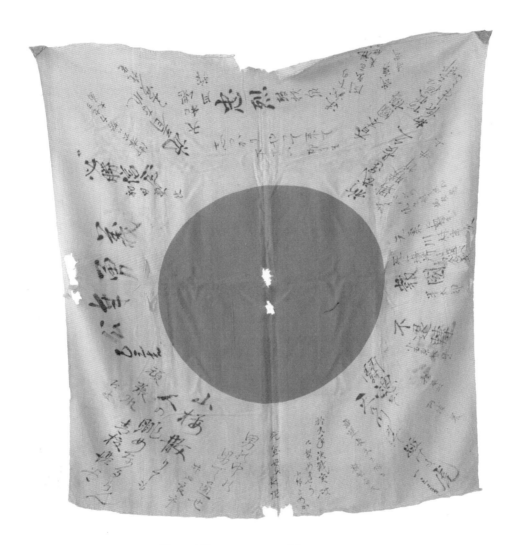

The Hinomaru Yosegoui
— the "Sun Round" —
sometimes known as the "Good Luck" flag
or the "sidways Writing" Banner

# 20

## HONORING DEATH: THE RISING SUN FLAG

*"One of the first Japanese soldiers I killed had a nice flag that I took out of his helmet and kept. It has several holes in it because my bullet struck him in the head."*

*"...."Fighting Spirit! A tiger running to the Milky Way"*—Jyu San Bu Tai

**MOST, IF NOT ALL, JAPANESE INFANTRYMEN CARRIED** a particular type of Japanese flag (the *Hinomaru Yosegui*) on their person. Those I knew about carried them in plastic, folded up in their helmet, to keep them clean and dry. All the ones that I have seen (hundreds!) have had writing in characters (Kanji) on the white background surrounding the red circle of the Rising Sun in the middle. I had always been led to believe that this was a sort of an informal service record of each soldier recorded on his flag.

One of the first Japanese soldiers I killed had a nice flag that I took out of his helmet and kept. It has several holes in it because my bullet struck him in the head—I have often said, "If I had known he had such a good flag, I would have aimed a little lower." I displayed and talked about this flag a number of times, and before I learned otherwise, I mistakenly spoke about "the service record" explanation of its purpose.

In 2006 when I was getting some DVDs of my "Veterans of the Valley" program duplicated, the person doing this gave me the name of a man at Texas A&M University who might be able to translate my flag.

I phoned George Adams, who graciously came to my home to see the flag and discuss the translation. George is fairly fluent in Japanese but his wife, Kazuko, was born in Japan and is even more fluent. He took the flag and they later presented me a dossier with all 25 of the messages translated. They even thanked me for giving them the privilege of seeing and translating the flag, even as I was trying to thank them!

The young Japanese soldier was named Sanshi (given name) Tomoe (family name) and was 19 when he was given the flag. (I was 19 when I shot him.) It turns out that the inscriptions are more like a yearbook signing at a going away party. Learning all that I did about Sanshi added a new dimension and poignancy to the flag.

Each of the messages is pessimistic about his survival and is signed by the writer. It is not clear whether these are family or friends. I never discovered where his home was where and when the signings occurred. The Japanese records are kept by Prefecture (similar to our state government), so you would have to know the answer before you could access his records.

The 25 messages and the writers' names are as follows:

Serve honorably—Tomoe Sanshi

Have faith that we will win—Wa Da Shige Nori

Do your utmost to serve—O Giku

Be calm—Mi Myo Yoshio

Japanese spirit—Tsuki Saku

We celebrate your departure for the final battle—Mi Ya Ko

Highest loyalty—Ko Ga Sen

Fight bravely—Yoshi Take

Please do your best—Yanagi Hara Sei

Japanese Imperial Flag—A Wa Toku Ji Ro

Pray and fight forever—Yanagi Sawa Han Zo

Pray for victory in war—Ino Ue

Avenge Saipan—Kaji Wara Kaname

I hope you are in good spirits—Kawa Mura Hun Ji

Choose the place where you will die—Taka Kura Gi Ichi

Serve your country—Han Ta Ko

Never give up—Ko Ishi Hara Ko No Gami

Serve—A Wa Sake

Fighting Spirit! A tiger running to the Milky Way—Jyu San Bu Tai

Pray forever for good fortune in battle—Kaji Wara Tora O

At 19, try hard to break through at the decisive battle—Ono Tomeka

Find the right death—Naga Sawa

Be a man—Inoue Yoichi

Cherry blossom falling but people stare (or: You will find honor in death)—Aoeda Goichi

Hang in there (or: Do your best)—Aki

The Japanese have a name for these distinctive signed battle flags: *Hinomaru Yosegoui*. This literally means "sun round" and "sideways writing". The rising sun flag is made out of silk, is 31 inches long by 28 inches wide, has never been cleaned, and is still slightly stained with the blood and brain matter of the soldier who carried it.

The Battlefield Cross — A Soldier's Memorial at Normandy
(Photo: National Archives — WWII)

# 21

## ON COMBAT, KILLING, AND FORGIVENESS

*"My conclusion and my belief is that God has forgiven me for taking human life in combat."*

**MY LIFE HAS BEEN A SPIRITUAL JOURNEY.** I will walk through it with you now to contrast my early status with my progress through life. I will also detail how my previous dates and girlfriends had little or no effect on me, whereas my relationship with Betty had a profound effect. On a scale of one to ten, as a Christian, I would say that it began at 0, moved to a plateau of 5–6, and moved up to a 9 and growing. I wouldn't say that I was an atheist, but was probably an agnostic. One of the few regrets I have is that I was not raised in a church-going family and did not read and study the bible when I was younger and could remember better.

My parents did not attend church and there were some other influences that turned me off to churches and organized religion. For example, what occurred when two Baptist churches in our block met together: one had a fire, and then met with the other, but the members of the destroyed church weren't allowed to take communion with the hosting church.

In 2015 we saw the chapel and cemetery in Vochriw, Wales (church of Wales – Anglican), where my paternal great grandparents would have gone to church (if they did) and taken my grandfather Elias. There was no known spiritual legacy from my parents or forbears.

My dad built and raced cars. His pride and joy was the "Blue Bell Special". He was in a very bad accident in Phoenix about 1921-1922. The doctors at the hospital said he was too bad off and they couldn't help him. Somehow they connected with the Christian Science Church, and the people prayed for him (and whatever else they do), and he survived to lead a normal life. Mom and Dad married in Phoenix, while he was in the hospital, January 1, 1923. He went on building racecars but he never raced again. Dad always had a soft spot in his heart for the Christian Science Church after that, but never participated in one. When my brother, Gil, and I were preschool age we were "sent" to a Sunday school at the Christian Science church, which was about two blocks from our home.

Later, when we were in elementary school, we were "sent" to Sunday school at the Congregational Church. My feeling was that if this was very important, Mom and Dad would have taken us and attended themselves. Therefore I didn't attach much significance to Sunday school or church and didn't get much out of it. Whenever they needed a minister (funeral, etc.), they used Charles Franklin Parker, pastor of the Congregational Church.

Gil joined the Boy Scout troop at the Congregational church but dropped out after a year or so. I joined the Boy Scout troop at the Methodist church and stayed active on into high school. The Troop attended services on "Scout Sunday" once a year as a troop!

My parents, later in life, started attending a Presbyterian church, but I don't know if either was baptized or joined.

My dad was a member of the Elks Lodge and one time I remember he was urged to start the "chairs" to move up through the leadership positions leading to Exalted Ruler. He was miserable and dropped out of the "chairs" after the first year. One of his duties was to give the invocation at some event and he asked me to help him write it–talk about the blind leading the blind!

My girlfriend in high school was a Methodist but she had no influence on me and my spiritual growth, even though she was a nice girl.

I would describe my lifestyle in high school as a "Dr. Jekyll and Mr. Hyde" one. On the good side I was heavily involved in school, ending up as president and valedictorian of my class (1944). I was editor of the school paper, business manager of the yearbook, in both Jr. and Sr. plays, National Honor Society and "15" club as both Junior and Senior. All this plus the Boy Scout activities.

Parallel to this lifestyle I also started the negative aspects of my life with drinking, smoking and swearing and other bad language. One incident/example that I recall was when I was about 12 and my brother Gil and two of his friends and classmates (all three about 14) and I went for a hike north of town. We came upon what appeared to be an abandoned ranch house. We rode a buggy downhill into the water tank, trashed the house, broke windows, and painted graffiti on the barn. Suddenly the ranch owner–Ed Weston–drove up, caught us, and took us to town in his pickup to the sheriff's office. He knew our dad and did not press charges. We were fined $25.00 each for damages, and one guy was "sentenced" by his parents to attend Sunday school for a year. He went reluctantly and I think it did more harm than good.

Another incident was in 1943. A friend and classmate worked part-time after school for the Atcheson, Topeka and Santa Fe railroad. One day he got hold of another classmate and me and said, "Get down here ASAP." A boxcar of wine had been damaged and wine was running out of the boxcar onto the ground. The local winos had gathered and were catching it in whatever vessels they could and slurping the rest. I would estimate that the boxcar was about half full of cases of Rose wine and that about 1/4 to 1/3 was broken. There were *lots* of bottles that were unbroken.

It turned out that the RR had to submit the labels off the bottles for insurance and were planning to destroy the broken and the unbroken bottles. The 3 of us got a washtub and filled it with water and soaked the labels off the bottles. We had cases and cases of Rose wine (in plain bottles without labels) and guzzled it for weeks until it ran out. I was about 16-17 years old and in my Junior year of high school.

This pattern continued on and grew when I went into the Army. After going into the Army at age 18, my language and drinking got worse but fortunately I never really got hooked on smoking. I knew the Army had chaplains and chapels but I never personally saw either.

Basic Infantry training was rugged and strenuous and we were "brain washed" to make us want to kill the enemy and avoid them killing us. Fort Ord, Fort Lewis and troop trainings were just more of the same.

Life on three troop ships and short stops on Oahu and Saipan were uneventful and nothing like combat on Okinawa. Whoever said, "There are no atheists in foxholes" sure knew what he was talking about and hit the nail on the head. Combat was enough to put the fear of God into anyone, and I had a feeling that God had a hand on me and that I was spared for something better.

After I was shot in the right foot on Okinawa, there followed 3 months of hospitalization and 2 surgeries in hospitals in Guam, Oahu, San Francisco and Modesto, CA where I dated a 2$^{nd}$ Lt. Army nurse from Canada. After release from the hospital and some leave, I was sent to Fort Sam Houston in San Antonio, TX. While there I was sent to the USAFI (United States Armed Forces Institute) headquarters at the University of Wisconsin in Madison, WI. While there I dated a Norwegian girl and also back in San Antonio I dated several girls casually. My drinking and foul language continued.

After my discharge from the Army I went to North Hollywood, CA, where my parents were living. I bought a well-used 1937 Ford Coupe and Dad and I (mostly Dad) worked it over and I then headed over to Tucson, AZ to enter the University of Arizona. I enrolled in a general business program in the College of Business and Public Administration. After my first semester I was given a job to grade papers for a class in Economic Geography, which I had aced. I also joined Alpha Kappa Psi, honorary business fraternity. From then on till graduation I spent Sunday mornings grading papers. Besides a heavy load of classes there was time for drinking and trips to Nogales, and also for dating Carol, then Kay and a few others. I graduated Cum Laude in 3 years with no summer school as I spent summers working in Prescott.

I never went to church until after I started dating Betty. I first met Betty in the fall of 1948 where she worked as secretary to Dean Brown in the Business College. She gave me my monthly check for my paper grading. I always said she sure didn't start dating me for my money! I thought she was cute and I enjoyed her Mississippi accent.

At mid-year enrollment our Alpha Kappa Psi fraternity, in which I served as president, assisted the BPA staff, and when we were through I helped Betty take stuff from Old Main back to the BPA College. I offered to give her a ride home. She lived at the YWCA about 6 blocks from campus. On the way we stopped by a local gathering place and she had a Coke and I had a beer. She let me know that she didn't drink nor approve of anyone else doing so!

One time in the late 1960s, Betty gave me a six-pack of beer as a stocking stuffer. I would never have guessed that one—you could have knocked me over with a feather! It stayed in the refrigerator for months and she finally asked me to drink it and get rid of it.

A few days later I called her up and asked her to go to a Tucson Symphony Orchestra concert in a couple of weeks. Before that event, I found out about another musical or play and made a 2$^{nd}$ date before we had had our first. My friends thought I was nuts, but I knew she was special.

From then on we started dating more and started going to the Methodist church on Sunday mornings. She had another boyfriend who owned an airplane and later dropped him and went out with me more. Betty never "preached" to me, but set an example of Christian living that was winsome. I realized that I wanted to share in what she had, the spiritual life she lived. This was also a turning point for me in regard to my drinking and bad language.

After graduation I took a job in Phoenix with the Arizona Five Rating Bureau. I commuted every weekend back and forth to Tucson to court my true love. She was under pressure to marry a guy in Mississippi who was studying to be a doctor and was a friend of the family. She finally broke that off and at Christmas 1949 we became engaged and decided to live in Dallas as a compromise, about halfway between Arizona and Mississippi.

I wanted to be with Betty and to "take" any children we might have to Sunday school and church. So, as an intellectual decision I was baptized at age 24 by Rev. John Shuler and joined Lakewood Methodist Church in Dallas. We were married at First Methodist Church, Columbia, MS on April 23, 1950 and Betty transferred her membership to Lakewood. I bought my first bible to have as a family bible. It was King James Version.

At first I worked for Firestone and Betty got a job at Minneapolis Honeywell. Later I was offered a Claims Representative position in a new social security office they were opening in Longview, TX. It wasn't ready yet so they had me EOD in the Tyler SSA office and start my training. Since our stay in Tyler was to be temporary, we visited Methodist churches there but didn't join.

While in Tyler I traveled some and found a plaster plaque in Overton which I liked, and I bought it:
"Christ is the head of this house,
   The unseen host at every meal,
   The silent listener at every conversation."

Later I bought another one and gave it to Betty's parents.

Our pastor at Lakewood knew a pastor in Longview and recommended Wesley Methodist Church when we got there. We joined Wesley Methodist Church in Longview with Compton Riley as our pastor. Our firstborn son, Lane, was born in Longview. We regularly attended Sunday school and church at Wesley.

Later I was promoted from Claims Representative to Field Representative and transferred to San Angelo, TX. We visited first Methodist Church but were invited to help start a new church on the west side of town–St. Luke's. I became more involved in the church than I had ever been, besides regular Sunday school and church. Both our two daughters were born in

San Angelo and baptized at St. Luke's. As our family grew we took them to the nursery and later to Sunday school. I painted a sign for the future site of St. Luke's and became close to the pastor, Morris Bratten and his family.

Betty's mother was a Methodist and her stepfather was Catholic. She sent us a copy of the Revised Standard Bible when it came out and it was easier to read and understand.

I was asked to teach an adult Sunday school class, and before I gave them an answer we went on a trip to Prescott. I fell asleep while driving near Pietown, New Mexico, right on the continental divide. We could all three have been killed but we survived with minor scratches and bruises. Once again I felt like God had spared me, and I felt a strong pull to call San Angelo and tell them I'd teach the class. There were no phones for hundreds of miles, and when I cooled down I decided I wasn't ready to teach.

Late in our time in San Angelo and as a result of some personnel changes I became the Officer in Charge and then promoted and transferred as Assistant District Manager in Austin, Texas. In Austin, where we stayed a couple of years, we went to Shettles Memorial Methodist Church. We attended regularly and Betty and I both taught children's Sunday school classes, but were not otherwise involved.

My job as Assistant District Manager in Austin was stressful and I hoped we wouldn't stay too long. It had been a transitional position and the several ahead of me had moved on fairly rapidly. After 2 ½ years I received another promotion and transfer to District Manager in Bryan, Texas. A friend at Shettles had relatives in Bryan and introduced us to them and St. Paul's Methodist Church. We liked the pastor, Gene Craig, and knew his sister at Wesley in Longview. Many years later Gene ended up at Memorial Drive UMC Houston and our son and family attended there. Gene baptized our grandson Brian at Memorial Drive.

St. Paul's was a small, but very active church and I became involved in many of the "business" activities: Administrative Board, Trustees, Education, missions, staff parish Treasurer (for 15 years), and Adult Sunday school class teacher.

The greatest thing at St. Paul's and certainly in my life was a "Lay Witness Mission" held in the spring of 1969. It had a profound effect on me, my family, and the church. A busy weekend started on Friday night and we had about 30 lay men and women from all over East Texas under the direction of coordinator, John Sparks. All shared about their

Christian lives and their relationship not only to the Methodist church but to Jesus Christ. All the visitors left Sunday afternoon and we had an Evaluation meeting in Fellowship Hall Sunday night. This was my job to plan, coordinate, MC, and record this meeting. I had a tape recorder but forgot to turn it on for the opening prayer. I thought about John Wesley and how his heart was strangely warmed at the Aldersgate experience: I too, felt very intimately the presence of Christ in me and with my feet two feet. off the floor, that I was a channel for God praying through me. After the prayer I remembered to turn on the tape recorder and got the rest recorded.

Everyone was excited and wound up and Coleman Lloyd, who had been out of town, wanted to know what was going on–he certainly could see the difference in St. Paul's.

The main activity was to organize small (not less than 4, not more than 6 couples) share groups. We ended up with every night of the week and some nights with multiple groups. Betty and I chose a Friday night group and we had:

| | | |
|---|---|---|
| Youngest | Brotherton | A&M undergrad (no children) |
| Middle | Norris | A&M graduate school, school teacher (no children) |
| Middle | Johnson | A&M Physical Plant (2 children) |
| Oldest | Rees | Social Security office (3 children) |

We rotated each week and so hosted the group about once a month. The host man was the leader for their meeting and we prayed, read, and discussed the bible, shared and had refreshments. A fond memory is of Caroline Johnson's chocolate sheet cake!

When I joined the church I think it was an intellectual act. I always felt like the Lay Witness Mission made it drop from my head to my heart.

Everyone had a burning desire to read (both the bible and books such as Barclay, Jones, Gothard, Schaeffer, Miller, Yancey, etc.). Many wanted to go on Lay Witness Missions to other churches to witness to the change in our lives and new intimate relationship with Jesus. I went to six missions in Bryan and as far away as Hughes Springs, near Daingerfield.

We bought William Barclay's Daily Study Bible, and several modern translations, and also books by E. Stanley Jones. Betty and I went to Dallas for the Bill Gothard crusade and to Houston to see and hear Francis and

Edith Schaeffer. We also met and heard Keith Miller and Phillip Yancey. There was also a rush to Precept and other bible studies.

Following the LWM I was convicted with the desire/need to tithe. At the time I was giving about 5%, Lane was starting at A&M that fall and Ann and Ellen were still in high school with college to come. I came up with a plan to up my giving 1% a year until I reached 10% of my net. Later I was led to make it 10% of my gross.

About 2-3 years after the LWM, Jim Keller was coming home from an out of town LWM and got a calling to start a prayer group for the men at St. Paul's. This was about 1971 or 1972; we have now been meeting each Tuesday and Thursday morning for over 40 years.

Another meaningful part of my life, not overtly religious but doing a lot of good locally and worldwide, has ben my involvement in the Rotary Club. I have been a member for 58 years, am a past president and 6 time Paul Harris Fellow. I look forward to our Wednesday noon meetings, which always begin with a prayer.

I never had any problem in high school, the army or part-time army before 21, in buying or obtaining tobacco products or booze. It always bothered me that when I was discharged from the army at age 20, I could be drafted to fight and get wounded but couldn't *legally* buy alcohol or vote!

All of this relating of my spiritual life, and lack thereof, lead up to how I resolved the two greatest moral and philosophical issues of my life:

1. Personal: killing the enemy in combat, soldier to soldier
2. National: the use of aerial bombardment, including nuclear weapons

The first point of conflict is the admonition in the 10 commandments that "Thou shall not kill". When, after the war, I came to question my role as a combat infantryman, I thought about God sending the flood, saving Noah but killing all the rest. The next lesson I found was how, when Moses and the Israelites fled Egypt, God parted the Red Sea, saving His people but killing the Egyptian forces pursuing them. In Matthew, the scripture says there will always be wars and rumors of war. Finally, in Acts 10:verse we read about the Roman centurion, I found the story of Cornelius and his household as an example of faith and living.

When I finally got my Japanese flag translated and found out the name of the first enemy soldier that I killed (Tomoe Sanshi, age 19, same as me) it added a whole new dimension of poignancy, a connection to the enemy I

TEMPORARY U.S. CEMETERY NEAR MABUNI, OKINAWA, AT THE END OF THE CAMPAIGN (U.S. ARMY PHOTO, CENTER OF MILITARY HISTORY, WASHINGTON D.C. — AS USED IN **OKINAWA: THE LAST BATTLE** BY ROY E. APPLEMAN, JAMES M. BURNS RUSSELL A. GUGELER, AND JOHN STEVENS)

had killed in combat. Tomoe Sanshi was a young soldier who fought for his nation and died for it. I was a young soldier who fought for my nation, was wounded for it. Unlike him, I went on to live a long and happy, productive civilian life. It was a lesson in the moral burden of killing in combat—fortunately for me, it was a lesson I was able to deal with and learn from after the fact.

My conclusion and my belief is that God has forgiven me for taking human life in combat. Once I knew I was forgiven, this particular incident became water under the bridge, and I was able move on to accomplish what I needed to live the life that God had planned for me.

In regards to the second issue, the effects of war on civilians: my opinion is that *no* war, no killing of anyone, civilian or military, is either good or desirable as an outcome. It's only justified as the last resort. It's also a matter of perspective. A massive number of people—men, women, children—were killed in the firebombing of Tokyo, but we don't talk about that. More people were killed in conventional fighting on Okinawa, including about 15,000 Americans and over 200,000 Okinawans and Japanese, than died at Hiroshima and Nagasaki combined. The projected killing, the death toll if we had attacked Japan as planned was up to be at

AN UNDATED IMAGE SHOWS HIROSHIMA AFTER THE ATOMIC BOMBING.
(PHOTO: HIROSHIMA PEACE MEMORIAL MUSEUM/EUROPEAN PRESSPHOTO AGENCY)

least one million American casualties, killed and wounded, and multiple *millions* of Japanese military and civilians.

We knew that the Axis was working on rockets and atomic weapons. If they had them they would surely have not hesitated to use them on us. An invasion of the Japanese home islands, even in victory, would have devastated both sides. Using those two atomic weapons ended the war, stopped the killing, and saved millions of Allied and Japanese lives.

I have had generally good health with a few exceptions:

| | |
|---|---|
| Malignant myopia | all my life |
| Gunshot wound | 1945 – 70+ years ago |
| Diabetes | age 55 – 35+ years ago |
| Abdominal surgery | 2006 |
| Heart valve, 1 bypass | 2014 |

My dear wife Betty had Alzheimer's the last 15 years of her life.

In all, I have lived a very blessed life. I fought, I killed, and I was wounded in combat, but with God's help, I survived. Afterward, I was forgiven, and I was given the right direction for my life. I believe that

God saved me in combat and he protected me and my family through the automobile accident because He had a plan for me. I have been blessed with sixty-three years of marriage, three children, five grandchildren, and ten great grandchildren. I have never been wealthy but have lived comfortably. My job with Social Security lasted thirty-seven years, including twenty-seven years as District Manager in Bryan—most of which I enjoyed. This has provided me with a good retirement and benefits.

I reached nintey years of age in January 2016—which means that I have lived longer than everyone in my family, and longer than most of my fellow infantrymen who fought in WWII.

CORNERSTONE OF PEACE — OKINAWA, JAPAN
(GNU CREATIVE COMMONS SHARE)

# American History

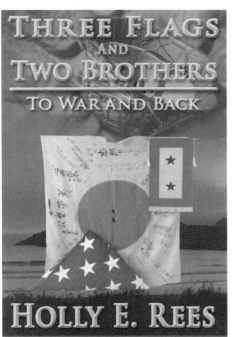
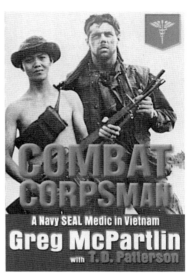

## *Revolution Combat Adventure* from Lone Star Publishing

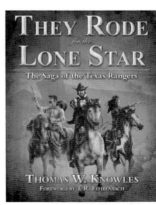

an imprint of Event Horizon Publishing Group

eventhorizonpg.com